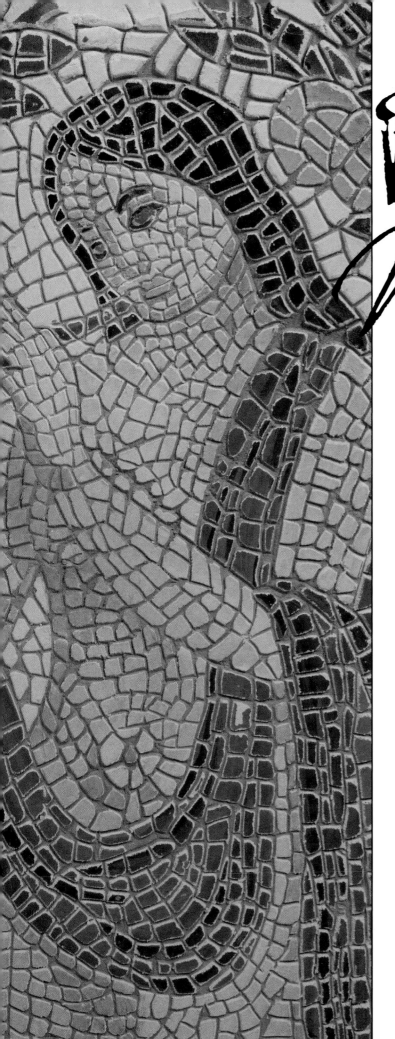

Flaster Mosaics

Kristin Peck

Published by

krause publications

700 East State Street • Iola, WI 54990-0001
715/445-2214 • FAX: 715/445-4087   www.krause.com

Please call or write for our free catalog of publications.
Our toll-free number to place an order or obtain a free
catalog is 800-258-0929, or please use our regular busi-
ness telephone 715-445-2214.

All photography by Joe Jacobs.

Library of Congress Catalog Number: 2002113121

ISBN: 0-87349-535-7

Dedication

To my boys, Ryan and Connor, who can drive me crazy; and to my husband, David, who keeps me sane. I think that's a pretty good balance.

Acknowledgments

Without the support of such a fine publishing house like Krause Publications and its amazing staff, this book would not be possible. Thank you Julie, Jodi, and the Krause art department. I have learned that although an author's deadline is a lot of work, the real work begins after it's written.

I would like to also thank the manufacturers who gave their total support during this project.

Plaid® Enterprises
Walnut Hollow®
Kemper Tools
FM Brush Co. Inc. (manufacturers of the Dynasty paint brush)
Silkpaint!® Corporation (manufacturers of the Air Pen)

A special thank you to Michaels® Arts and Crafts, Elmer Baggott, Pam Hawkins, Veronica Towey, Sandy Bares, Lauren Powell, Katie Munday, Michele Hester, Beth McCleery, and my photographer, Joe Jacobs.

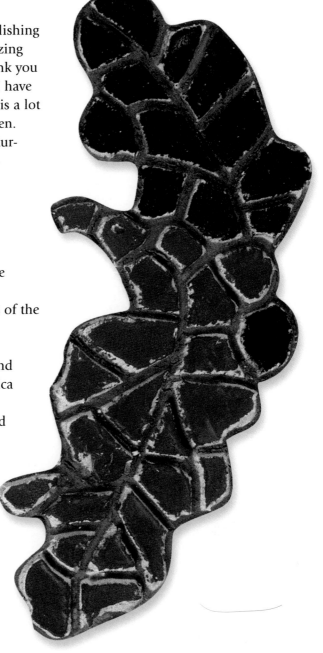

Table of Contents

Introduction

The word *mosaic* conjures up many images, from a faded fountain among the ruins of Italy to the glass and steel mosaics found in modern public buildings. Today we recognize the time and commitment that goes into creating a mosaic, and these pieces have become symbols of luxury. Historically, mosaics were more prevalent. They were mainly used to embellish architecture, but their pictorial compositions were later used to embellish floors, fountains, and even furniture. The history of mosaics is riddled with artistry that repeats itself and evolves from one period to another. From ancient Babylon, where mosaics were created from semi-precious stones, shells, and bits of pottery, to contemporary artists who use cement and metal in their mosaic work, mosaics have been a popular form of self-expression. Each period has its own unique perspective, and each period represents the values and artistry of its time.

The earliest mosaics were created by ancient civilizations using pebbles or shells. The designs were simple, abstract, and usually consisted of two colors. Later more colors were introduced, but the simplicity of the design usually dominated the surface. Mosaics became an effective and resourceful means of paving floors and walkways. Because of their endurance, both physically and artistically, mosaic arts continue to thrive even in today's world.

One of the greatest galleries of mosaic art lies at the feet of Mount Vesuvius. With the entombment of Pompeii came the salvation of some of the most moving and awe-inspiring mosaics the world has ever seen. What is it about a mosaic that lures the observer to investigate

what our eyes tell us? We're drawn closer until we can see that this is not made up of one piece, but of many fragments that create a whole. No two alike, mimicked but never duplicated, the concept has inspired artists from every medium to create mosaics from just about everything.

In the past, we have had to gaze at mosaics from behind the glass of a museum or from a distance as we watch some unattainable TV program heralding the splendors of the rich and famous. With *Plaster Mosaics*, we will now be able to enjoy the beauty of mosaics without the expense of obtaining them. Plaster mosaics are affordable, easy to do, and limitless in their applications. What would have taken a mosaic artist two weeks to accomplish will take you two hours. What would have cost that same mosaic artist hundreds if not thousands of dollars in materials will cost you only a few dollars.

As this is a new technique, your creations will truly be one of a kind. In addition to having something unique, there's no standard against which to compare your work. This means that no one will notice a mistake, because there's no precedent for that mistake. You will be the creator of a work of art that will appear as if it was taken from the villa walls of Pompeii.

Step-by-step instructions will build the skills needed to apply your plaster mosaic art to just about any surface. From these projects, you will be able to alter, add, or create your own technique or style. I encourage you to explore all of the possibilities this technique has to offer.

Classical mosaic art by Irina Charny.

Introduction

to Color

When we look at anything, whether it's a car, a piece of furniture, or even a flower, we all notice one thing first—color. After color comes pattern and then texture. Because color is first, it's the one thing that will make or break a project. For example, when we view a painting and the color is horrible, we turn away. It's difficult to move past the color to see what the painting was all about. Color affects us physically, emotionally, and spiritually. It has a direct effect on our moods and perceptions, whether they are good or bad.

The psychology of color has been studied for years, and its lessons are incorporated into our everyday lives. Hospitals are swathed in soothing shades of pastel to create a calming atmosphere. Retail stores, on the other hand, use bright intense colors to create excitement and a sense of urgency. Lively warm colors draw us near, excite us, and fill us with happiness. Grays or black introduce a mood of quiet and soberness. No matter what the subject matter, you can create a mood by choosing certain colors.

When creating a plaster mosaic, it's important to choose your colors wisely. The good news is that no matter what you decide, it can be changed at any time. It's only a matter of choosing the color and picking up your brush. But for argument's sake and the desire to get it right the first time, you need to know why color plays such a major role in mosaics.

When you look at an intricate mosaic, you are given the impression of shades of color or, more to the point, an illusion of colors that transition into one another. In fact, a mosaic is made up of fixed pieces of color that create the movement from one color to another. It's designed much like a painting. The artist chooses the colors to create the illusion of depth, motion, and mood, but, in many paintings, colors appear blended and fluid up close *and* from a distance. With a mosaic, up close it's obvious that the colors are individual pieces. It's only when you move back that the colors appear unified. With a true mosaic piece, you have a fixed color. What you see is what you get.

With the plaster mosaic technique, your palette is unlimited, and you can change your colors as often as you wish. Understanding the fundamentals of color will make it easier to plan your mosaic. It's always easy to pick your favorite color from a choice of five colors, but when you are faced with a palette of infinite choices, it becomes very difficult. In the following pages, we will break it down so your choices are not only easier but they will allow you better success with your projects.

Color Basics

Remember that black and white are not considered colors, but are still incorporated into our color palette.

The Color Wheel is a visual organization of colors and how they relate to each other. It's built upon itself, starting with the three primary colors—yellow, blue, and red.

Have you ever noticed how nature has used the color wheel to its best advantage? Amazingly enough, when you see an exotic bird with plumage made of a half dozen colors, it never clashes. Flowers, birds, trees, and even the rocks along a riverbed make the best of colors. Faced with a color wheel, how do we decide which colors match and work with each other? The following terms will give you a basic look at how colors work with each other.

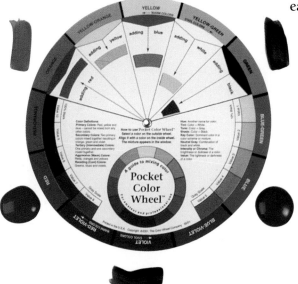

"The Color Wheel"
Pocket Color Wheel
(The Color Wheel Company)

Hue—The name of a color is its hue. If you were talking about blue and yellow, you would be distinguishing them by one as being a blue hue and the other a yellow hue.

Value—Value is the lightness or darkness of a color.

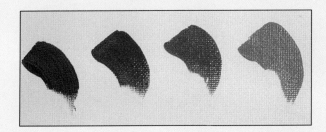

Primary colors—Yellow, Blue, and Red are the primary colors and the basis for every other color. They cannot be created by mixing colors.

Secondary Colors—Secondary colors are made by mixing two adjoining primary colors. An example would be mixing yellow with blue, which gives you green. There are three secondary colors: green, purple, and orange.

Tertiary Colors—Tertiary colors are obtained by mixing a primary color with an adjacent secondary color. Mixing red (primary) with orange (secondary), will give you red-orange. There are traditionally 12 colors on a color wheel, which can be broken down further to create other colors.

Complementary Colors—Complementary colors are any two colors directly across from each other on the color wheel.

Monochromatic Colors—Monochromatic colors begin with one color. White is then used to lighten the color, and black is used to shade it.

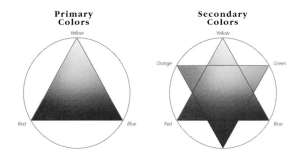

Tint—By adding white, we tint the color and lighten its value.

Shade—By adding black, we not only change the value, but we alter the hue.

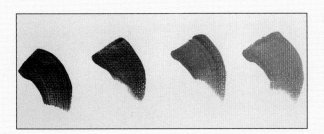

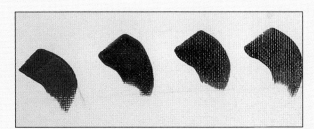

The Basic

Creating plaster mosaics is not only easy, it's very inexpensive. For years, I've admired the intricacies of mosaic composition. After spending both time and money, I learned two things: One, I wanted instant gratification, which you don't get with mosaics no matter how small the project. And two, it's very expensive to buy the components for a mosaic project even if it's the size of a coaster. I learned that I didn't have the patience or the skill to sit down and create what I saw in my mind.

The technique for plaster mosaics was created the same way a lot of things are—by doing something totally unrelated without any expectations for what the final result may be. I was taking a painting class at a local community college a few years back. The class covered many paint techniques, from sponging and gilding to painting frescos. For the final, I needed one complete project, and since I was going to miss the last class, my instructor gave me homework that would qualify. We spoke for

Tools

five minutes, and knowing my propensity toward working with tile, he challenged me to come up with a way to imitate a tile mural.

I spent seven hours on the first piece. That night my kids ate peanut butter and jelly, because I was afraid to stop. As most artists know, once you're on a roll, the walls can come tumbling down around you and you wouldn't notice. What I did realize was that I found a way to create exquisite pieces with a fraction of the labor and a fraction of the cost. After many hours of experimentation, plaster mosaics was born.

Working with plaster mosaics will require very few items or specialized tools. The following pages will walk you through the most important materials, and a general instruction to the technique follows. Other specialized tools are added and discussed as the projects increase in complexity.

Plaster Compound—The plaster compound is the actual material that you will use to create the mosaic. This material is your run-of-the-mill, store-bought, pre-mixed joint compound. It's the stuff you use to plaster drywall joints and fill in the nail pops on your living room wall. It comes in a resealable container and in different sizes from one quart up to a five-gallon pail. It's an amazing fluffy white material that can be sanded, carved, molded, and painted. I don't recommend any particular brand, because they all basically work the same. I do however recommend that

(Left to Right) The Basics: putty knives, bucket of plaster compound, measuring spoons, sandpaper, Popsicle stick, masking tape, disposable cup.

▶ **tip** **U**se clear plastic cups, so you can see at a glance what color compound you mixed.

▶ **tip** **C**over your mixed compound by simply pulling a piece of plastic wrap over the cup and stirrer. Just punch the stick right through the plastic wrap.

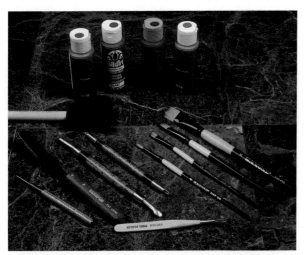

(Clockwise from top) Acrylic paints, assorted paint-brushes, wire loop carving tools, palette knife, finger tool, disposable sponge brush.

it be fresh, because any dried pieces will show up as lumps in the application.

The majority of the projects in this book are made with interior grade joint compound, but there is an exterior grade joint compound. It's intended for exterior wall cracks or mortar and stucco cracks. Although it needs to be sealed, it's manufactured to withstand exterior conditions better than the interior grade. Regardless, I still recommend your finished project be placed in a sheltered outside area. The exterior compound has the same mixing and application characteristics, while giving you the opportunity to expand the uses of your plaster mosaic.

Substrate—The substrate is the surface on which you will stage your mosaic. Because of the plaster compound's versatility, your substrate can be wood, mason or clay products, wallboard, canvas board, or anything with a porous surface.

Color—I use two types of acrylic mediums: pigments and paint. Most of the pigments are mixed directly into the plaster compound. Pigments are more intense, concentrated colors, which allow you to add a little and have it go a long way. By adding small amounts of pigment to the plaster compound, you avoid watering it down too much. Runny plaster is more difficult to manipulate and will crack during the drying process. Acrylic paints, in most cases, are used for decorative painting. The coverage is adequate, the applications smooth, and they dry quickly.

Carving Tools—Carving tools are very essential components of the process. Although I may recommend specific tools throughout the book, you will find that some tools work better than others. Wire tools are essential, because they carve out the plaster while allowing it to pass through the tool. A wire tool with an edge not only pulls the plaster away from your piece, it also cuts into plaster that has started to dry without crumbling it.

Palette and Putty Knives—Most hardware stores carry an array of putty blades. I recommend the inexpensive plastic putty knives in a range of sizes. If you do decide on a putty knife with a metal blade, remember that the smallest speck of plaster compound or water left on the blade will cause it to rust. The plastic brands work just as well and last longer with minimal care. Purchase narrow knives for small applications, and a wide blade for smooth applications on large expanses of area.

Palette knives are found in the art departments of most art and hobby supply stores. They are ideal for smoothing out the top on a project and for the base coat on projects with hard to reach areas. Because of the bend in the handles, you can reach areas that you would not be able to reach with a putty knife.

Sandpaper—Sandpaper plays an important role throughout the plaster mosaic process. You will need two types: fine grit and medium grit. Fine sandpaper is used during the finishing stage of plaster mosaics. It creates a smooth finished surface, while only taking off minute amounts of plaster. You can also use fine sandpaper to create an antique effect by gradually taking off small amounts of paint and giving it a worn look.

Medium grit is usually used on the base coat of plaster. It's used to quickly take down high areas, ridges, or surface irregularities. Because it takes down the plaster quickly, it creates a lot of dust, so it's best to use the medium grit outside.

If you need to sand a very large area, like an entire wall, you could wrap a sheet of sandpaper around a sanding block to more evenly sand out your surface. Sanding with your fingers may cause ridges where your fingers applied more pressure than the area between your fingers. A sanding block also makes sanding large areas easy and quick.

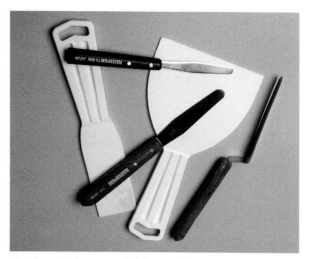
Plastic putty knives and different shaped palette knives.

Medium and fine grit sandpaper.

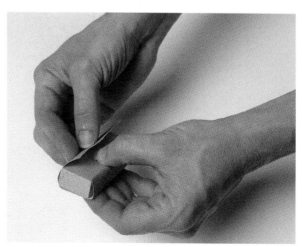
Rolling a piece of sandpaper around a small block of wood allows you to apply even level pressure over your surface, giving you a smooth plane.

The mosaic on the left is coated with a gloss varnish, while the one on the right is coated with matte varnish. Applying a sealer will intensify the colors.

Sealers and Varnishes—For any
plaster mosaic on wood, you will need to use a wood sealer at the beginning of the project and a final sealer at the end. Water-based sealers cause the grain of the wood to rise. This is actually the wood swelling because the water in the sealer is being drawn into the grain. I recommend that you lightly sand the surface and apply a second coat of sealer before you add the base coat of plaster. Although the project will be covered in plaster and you will never notice if the surface is actually smooth or sealed, it ensures that the pores in the wood are closed. If the wood is porous, the moisture in the plaster will be drawn out too quickly. This will cause the plaster to dry prematurely, leaving you with less time to work on your project.

Sealing the wood is also important because the plaster compound has water in it, which will be drawn into unsealed wood like a sponge. Because the water is drawn out of the plaster so quickly, it will start to crack and crumble. Also, sealing your wood prior to starting your project allows you to paint areas that you decide not to cover with plaster mosaics.

A top sealer is used to protect your work and to complement the style of your work. If you wanted to mimic the look of china, you would use a high gloss varnish. If your piece was in the old world style of mosaics, you would use a matte or satin varnish to imitate old marble or granite. The same rule goes for your finishes throughout the book. If you were doing a faux marble table top, you would seal it in a high gloss varnish, which will not only bring out the color, but it will also reflect light like highly polished marble.

If you are going to use your project outdoors, you will need to use good quality polyurethane. Find one with UV protection to keep colors from fading, and re-apply it periodically.

Brushes—Brushes play an important role in the creation of plaster mosaics. For the most part, bristles should be very soft and pliable. Round and liner brushes are great for painting detail and grout joints. Wash and chisel brushes are used for painting large areas of the mosaic. Small filbert and chisel blenders, and shader brushes, are great for painting each individual mosaic piece.

Basic Tools—Everyday household items are also important tools. Disposable cups and plates allow you to mix your colors and then throw the whole thing away when you're done. Metal measuring spoons are preferred over plastic because they clean up so well. Popsicle sticks are ideal mixing tools, and old measuring cups or the scoop out of a coffee can make great measuring tools.

(From left to right) Round brush, liner brush, wash brush, large chisel brush, shader brush, chisel blender brush.

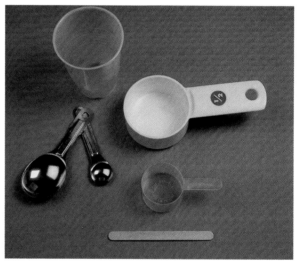

(From left to right) Disposable cup, metal measuring spoons, old measuring cup, scoop out of a coffee can, Popsicle stick.

tip▶Buy some Popsicle sticks and keep them on hand for mixing sticks.

General Instructions

These instructions are the fundamental steps used to complete a basic mosaic. From these steps, you will be able to build more advanced skills for future projects. It's very important to remember that these instructions are only general and that variations of techniques are introduced throughout the book. Before starting a project, read carefully through the instructions. Each project has variations that make it different from the last, and additional tools and materials may be required.

Preparing to Create Your Mosaic

Before you start a plaster mosaic, you must consider your work area.

- Plaster can make a considerable mess in both its wet and dry form, so spread out newspaper during the plaster application. This will make the clean-up process easy. Just roll up the mess after the work is complete.
- Sanding should be done outside, because of the dust that will be generated. Breathing plaster dust poses a serious health risk and should not be taken lightly.

- If you apply the plaster outside, avoid doing so in direct sunlight. The sun will dry out the plaster too quickly, giving you a crumbly texture to carve into.
- If you have completely carved your design and you're in a hurry to move on, set your project in the sun or in front of a fan to hurry the drying process. This will allow you to sand that much sooner.

Opposite: "Lady with Flute," see pattern on page 124.

Small Canvas

PRACTICE PROJECT

The mosaic that's pictured throughout this chapter was intentionally designed for demonstration purposes. The mosaic substrate is a 4" x 6" pre-primed artist's canvas.

▼ YOU WILL NEED

- 4" x 6" pre-primed artist's canvas
- 1 cup plaster compound
- Artist's pigment: Pure Black, Burnt Sienna, Raw Sienna*
- Artist's paint: Autumn Leaves*
- Wire tool*
- Brushes: liner, filbert*
- Putty knife
- Medium and fine grit sandpaper
- Waxed paper
- Measuring spoons, disposable cups, Popsicle sticks, paper plate

* Used in this project: Plaid paint, pigments; Kemper wire tool; Dynasty brushes.

▲**1.** In a disposable cup, use a Popsicle stick to mix 2 tablespoons of plaster compound with 1/2 teaspoon of Pure Black pigment until the color is well blended. Except where noted, colors should always be completely mixed into the plaster.

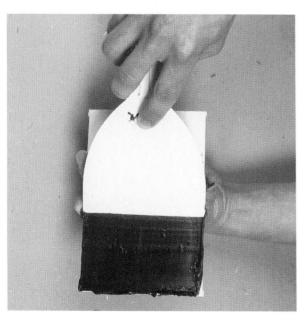

Using steady pressure while spreading the plaster in one movement will give you a smooth surface.

◀**2.** Using the putty knife and starting at the top of the artist's canvas, spread an even layer, approximately ⅛" thick, over the entire surface. With even pressure, pull the knife over the surface to ensure smooth coverage. If the surface appears jagged, or the coverage uneven, you can go over it a second time. This coating of plaster will appear between the carved pieces and will represent the grout joint. If the base coat were tinted white, you would have a white grout joint.

Allow the base coat to completely dry before moving on to the next step. Depending on the wetness of the plaster compound, the thickness it was applied, and the general room conditions, the base coat could dry in two hours or 24 hours. To determine whether the base coat is dry or not, touch it with the tips of your fingers. If it feels cold to the touch, it's still damp. Your base coat, especially if it's dark gray, will lighten up a shade or two. It's also important not to force dry your base coat, because the rapid drying will cause cracks in the surface.

tip ▶ It's always a good idea to use acrylic paint to base coat the object with the same color as the plaster base coat. This way, if you do carve beneath the plaster base coat, it will not be noticeable.

3. Once the base coat is dry, use the medium grit sandpaper to sand off bumps, jagged edges, or surface inconsistencies. Always use a light hand when sanding, so the sandpaper does not go through the base coat.

Sand with a light touch, taking a little off at a time.

tip

Always wear a mask or sand in a well-ventilated area. Sanding the base coat produces a large amount of fine dust particles, which could be harmful if inhaled.

▼ Applying the top coat

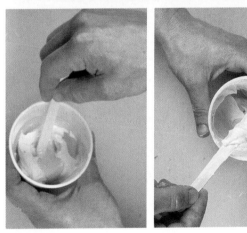

4. In a new disposable cup, mix 2 tablespoons of plaster compound with ⅛ teaspoon of Raw Sienna pigment until the color is well blended. The top coat color is the color your tiles will appear.

A small amount of pigment will go a long way toward tinting the plaster.

tip

If you mix the top coat Ivory and then paint the tile a darker color, the body of the piece will show through, which is what a glazed ceramic tile looks like. The body of the ceramic tile is usually white, while the glaze is a different color. When you chip a tile, you can see the white of the tile.

Apply the top coat with the same motion as the base coat.

5. With a clean putty knife, spread a ⅛" thick coating of Raw Sienna plaster compound over your base coat. It's important to keep the thickness of this coat as even as possible.

Allow the top coat to firm up. To determine whether or not it's ready, touch it with your fingertip. If you touch it and your finger comes away with plaster, it's too wet. If it feels soft but your finger comes away clean, it's ready to carve. The plaster can take between five and ten minutes to firm up, depending on how wet it is when you apply it. If it's a big project, it's better to do it in sections or keep it covered with plastic wrap, lightly draped over the piece, while you are working on it. The key is to plan ahead so you are not working against the clock.

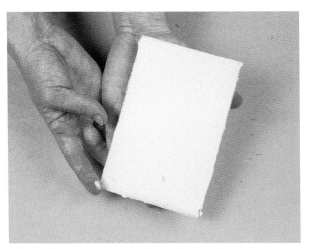

Plaster that's too wet is sticky to the touch.

Plaster that's ready to carve is like frosting that has been sitting out for a few minutes. The surface is slightly dry, but still soft, and it will indent when lightly pressed.

tip ▶ If you mix the top coat with a pigment that matches the color of the final piece, it will appear as if the color runs through the piece. This mimics marble, granite, and stone, which are colored throughout the body.

6. Copy the design on page 25, and secure it on a flat surface. Place a piece of waxed paper over the design, taping it down to keep it in place.

At this point, you can copy the design exactly, embellish it, or just draw simple guidelines. Use the liner to trace the design with a dark paint. Work quickly and use enough paint, so it will stay damp for transfer. It's important to remember that accuracy and neatness are not an issue at this point. These lines are only a guideline and will be covered up in the final project.

Load the brush and apply enough paint to keep it wet, so it will transfer onto the plaster.

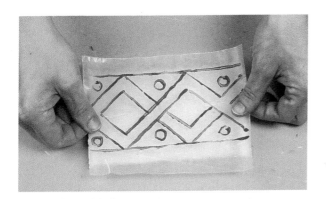

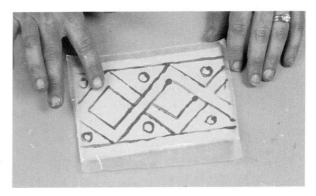

7. Quickly turn the waxed paper over onto the surface, and use a finger to trace the lines. Use a very light finger to transfer the wet paint onto the surface.

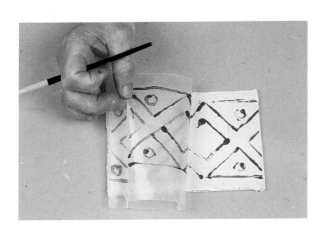

8. Gently grab a corner, and peel the waxed paper back.

Any lines that have not transferred can quickly be drawn in with the liner brush.

▲ **9.** Use a paper plate as a palette, and apply a small amount of Burnt Sienna and Autumn Leaves. With a filbert brush, quickly paint in the design. Again, neatness is not a priority with plaster mosaics.

tip **Variation for Transferring Your Design**

Transfer your design to a piece of paper. Newsprint works well because it is thin. Gently lay the paper on the plaster surface with the design facing up. Use the stylus to trace over the design. After the design is traced, gently pull the paper up, revealing the outline. Detail is not as important as getting the basic outline.

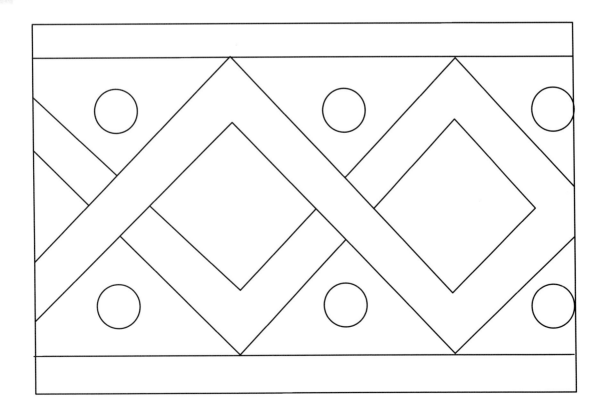

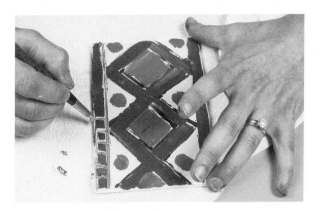 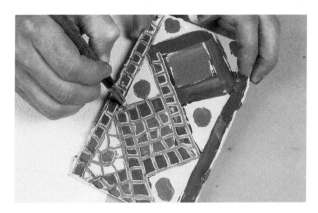

▲ **10.** Use a wire tool to carve through the top coat and reveal the base coat. To make rows of tile, carve two parallel lines and then carve those into individual tiles.

Work quickly, one section at a time, until the basic pieces are carved.

Allow the piece to completely dry before moving on to the next step. If you attempt to work on a damp piece, it will start to crumble.

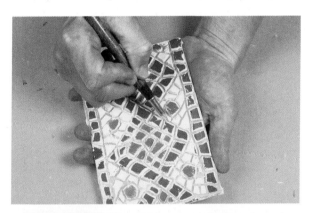

◀ **11.** Once the piece is dry, use the wire tool to clean out plaster from between the pieces. Plaster comes out easily once it has completely dried. This is the time to complete pieces that were not entirely carved, carve extra pieces, or change pieces that you're not satisfied with.

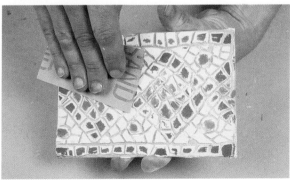

◀ **12.** Use the fine grit sandpaper to gently sand the ridges caused by the wire tool. The key to sanding is to take a little off at a time.

tip **C**lean the wire tool periodically with a paper napkin to take off any plaster buildup.

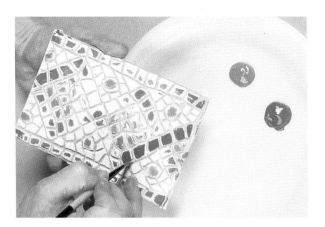
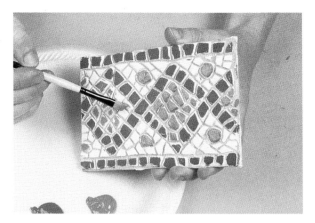

△ 13. Use the filbert or chisel brush to paint over any part of the design that was sanded off. A brush with a flat side allows you to paint over the pieces without getting the paint into the grout joints. At this point, you can completely change colors by painting over the original colors, or you can add colored pieces that were not there in the original design plan.

▼ Finishing the project

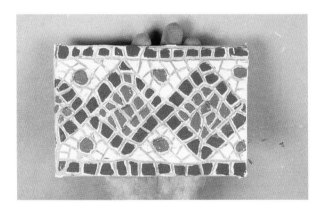

◀ 14. Once the project has completely dried, seal with varnish.

▼ Cleaning up after your plaster mosaic

- Roll up your newspaper and throw it away.
- If the plaster is still wet, wipe off your tools with paper towels, and wash off the residue with soap and water.
- If the plaster has dried on your tools, crumble the excess plaster off, and then rinse with water.

- Remember to dry your tools before putting them away. This will keep them from rusting.
- Do not throw lumps of plaster down your drain, or your plumber will have a new best friend. If you do not want to put wet plaster in your trash, dump it on some newspaper, let it dry, and then throw it away.

Decorative

Beyond the basic techniques and materials, there is a facet of plaster mosaics that enables each artist to imbibe his or her own distinctive style into its creation. All plaster mosaics are one of a kind, but taking advantage of different decorative effects will give you a mosaic with attitude. Because the basic ingredient to a plaster mosaic is the same surface material that you will find on your walls, it is an ideal surface for paint. This book covers only a handful of effects that can be used with paint and other store-bought materials. The best approach to creating unique decorative effects is to say that anything goes.

Mosaic Patterns

You can use the suggested patterns when you carve your mosaics, or try something that's more your style. In traditional mosaics, pieces are laid in specific patterns that vary the appearance of the same piece. The term describing these varied patterns is *opus*, which means *work* in Latin.

The mosaic pattern illustrated in this photo is *opus circumactum*. The background pieces are laid in a circular fan shape.

Effects

This mosaic pattern is *opus vermiculatum*. Notice the way the pieces flow, taking the shape of the form. *Opus vermiculatum* give the effect of movement and elegance. They are seen in many classical mosaics.

Opus regulatum is seen in today's manufactured mosaic sheets, where the pieces are lined up in straight rows. This is a very simple way to lay your pieces. You can add interest by shifting the direction of the mosaics used in the focus element, as seen in this photo.

Stencil Cutting

Using stencils with your mosaics is a good way to repeat your favorite designs throughout the mosaic. Whether you use the pre-made designs available at craft stores or choose to create your own, stencils help give your mosaic a professional look.

Stencil cutter.

▲**1.** Tape the pattern down to secure it.

▲**2.** Tape a stencil blank over the pattern.

▲**3.** Use a permanent marker to trace the design. Once the design is complete, remove the pattern from beneath the stencil blank and tape the stencil to a heat resistant surface.

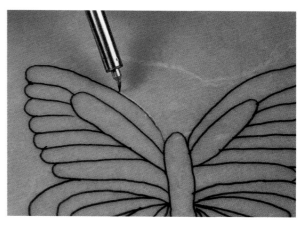

4. Following the manufacturer's directions, use even pressure to move the heated tip of the stencil cutter over the pattern. The stencil cutter will melt through the plastic blank.

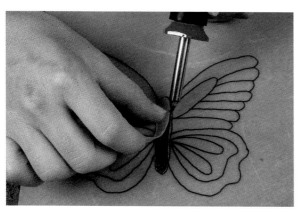

5. Pull out the cut pieces. If the pieces do not come out easily, use the stencil cutter to cut any areas that are still attached.

Marbleizing

Green Marble

This simple painting technique adds a touch of class to your mosaics. It can completely change the look of the piece. Use it to take your project from nice to extraordinary.

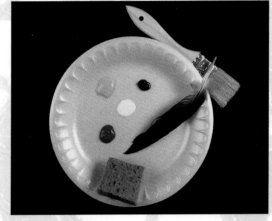

Marbleizing tools.

▼ YOU WILL NEED
- Artists' paints: Tartan Green, Summer Sky, Licorice, Wicker White*
- Thickener and extender
- Sponge Brush
- 2" disposable brush
- "Prepared" sponge
- Feather
- Fine sandpaper
- Paper plate

*Used in this project: Plaid paints.

1. With the sponge brush, paint the surface with two coats of Licorice, sanding between coats.

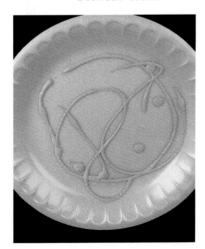

2. Swirl Tartan Green, Summer Sky, thickener, and extender onto a paper plate. Lift one edge of the plate, and slightly blend the colors.

▲**3.** Prepare the sponge by tearing off small pieces along the edge. This will eliminate the sharp edges.

▲**4.** Use a "prepared" sponge to apply the first layer of marble color. Press the sponge in a random pattern, slightly overlapping the previous pressing.

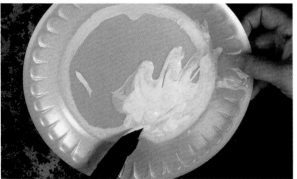
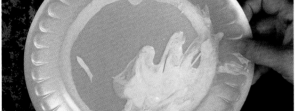

5. On a clean paper plate place a dab of Wicker White, extender, and thickener. Swirl them together.

◀**6.** Run the edge of the feather through the Wicker White paint.

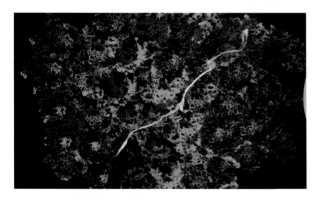

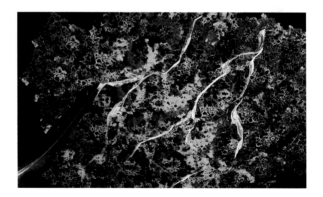

▲**7.** Feather in the veining using Wicker White. Keep the veins running in the same direction, and twirl the feather between your fingers to give the veining a natural movement.

◀**8.** Once the paint has started to dry, and is slightly tacky, use the disposable brush to lightly dry brush the veins to soften the lines.

Door Hanger

Door Hanger

Reminiscent of stained glass motifs, this door hanger is very easy to do and greets guests with a cheery welcome.

Variations on this door hanger could include a child's name, a playful "Do Not Disturb" sign, or you could create a door hanger for every holiday and express your good cheer through seasonal reminders.

▼ **YOU WILL NEED**
- Balsa wood door hanger
- Plaster compound
- Artist's pigment: Pure Black, Cobalt*
- Artist's paint: Metallic Amethyst, Plum, Christmas Green, Peridot*
- Matte sealer
- Wire tool*
- Brushes: small chisel brush*
- Medium grit sandpaper
- Putty knife

*Used in this project: Plaid paint and pigments; Kemper wire tool; Dynasty Brushes.

Review General Instructions, page 18, before beginning this project.

1. For the base coat, mix 2 tablespoons of plaster compound with ½ teaspoon of Pure Black pigment until the colors are well blended.

2. Use the putty knife to spread a ⅛" base coat evenly over the surface of the door hanger. Let dry completely before proceeding.

3. Use the medium grit sandpaper to sand the surface and all of the edges smooth.

4. For the top coat, mix 2 tablespoons of plaster with ½ teaspoon of Cobalt pigment until the colors are well blended.

5. Use the putty knife to spread a ⅛" top coat evenly over the base coat. Use the pallet knife to spread the plaster in one stroke over the bottom of the door hanger. It is easier to apply a few dabs of plaster around the doorknob opening, and then smooth it out. Allow the top coat to firm up for a minute or two before proceeding.

6. Transfer the design on page 36 to the surface. You may use either technique shown in the General Instructions.

7. Use the small chisel brush to paint in the design with the metallic colors. Metallic colors intensify with a second coat of paint.

8. Use the wire tool to carve out the design, exposing the black base coat. Keep the lines smooth and unbroken, pulling the tool straight up to end a line.

9. With the wire tool, freehand the word "Welcome," on the door hanger. "Welcome" can follow the curve of the doorknob opening, or it can be carved straight across. If free hand is not an option, computer-generated fonts can be used to try different looks. You can transfer fonts the same way you would transfer any other design.

10. Allow the surface to dry, and sand any inconsistencies, bumps, or ridges along the carved grout lines.

11. Touch up any paint that was sanded off, and seal with a matte sealer.

A variation on the "Welcome" door hanger could be a cheery holiday reminder.

Sun and Moon

Sun and Moon

One of the easiest ways to create interesting plaster mosaics is to use the pre-cut wood shapes found at hobby and craft stores. You can cover the entire shape with mosaics or just embellish it. These two pieces were done with two slightly different techniques to add contrast.

▼ **FOR THE MOON YOU WILL NEED**
- Wood moon shape
- Plaster compound
- Artist's paint: Blue Sapphire*
- Silver leaf
- Silver leaf adhesive
- Clear spray sealer
- Water-based wood sealer
- Brushes: large mop brush, chisel brush*
- Sponge brush*
- Wire tool*
- Small palette knife
- Fine grit sandpaper
- Masking tape, pencil, scissors

*Used in this project: Plaid paint; Dynasty brushes; Kemper wire tool.

▼ **FOR THE SUN YOU WILL NEED**
- Wood sun shape
- Plaster compound
- Artist's paint: Barnyard Red, Metallic Copper*
- Water-based wood sealer
- Clear spray sealer
- Spray stencil adhesive
- 6" x 6" sheet of paper
- Brushes: filbert, liner*
- Wire tool*
- Circle template or glass that fits your sun, leaving a ½" border
- Small palette knife
- Medium grit sandpaper
- Scissors

*Used in this project: Plaid paint; Dynasty brushes; Kemper wire tool.

Review General Instructions, page 18, before beginning this project.

The Moon

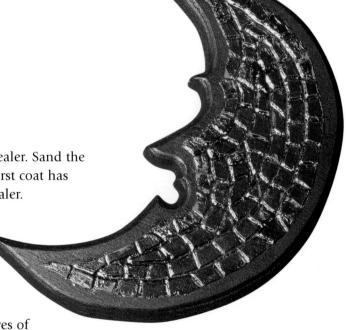

1. Seal the wood with a water-based sealer. Sand the surface with fine grit sandpaper after the first coat has dried, and apply a second coat of wood sealer.

2. Paint the moon with two coats of Blue Sapphire paint to ensure good coverage.

3. Use a pencil to outline the moon ¼" to ½" from the edge, following the curves of the moon. This will be the guideline for the masking tape.

4. Mask the rim of the moon with small pieces of masking tape, approximately an inch long. Use the pencil line as a guide. Press each piece of tape firmly down before adding the next piece of tape.

5. For the contoured areas of the face, take small pieces of tape and use scissors to cut out curves where the nose, forehead, and mouth are.

6. Use your small palette knife to spread approximately 1 tablespoon of plaster compound over the center of the moon, about 1/8" thick. Spread the plaster until it barely covers the inside edge of the tape. This project doesn't need tinted plaster, so the plaster can be used straight from the container.

7. Starting at the top of the moon, immediately peel the masking tape away from the surface. Pull the tape in a clean upward motion. If a piece breaks away, grasp it at the top, and pull it off in the same upward motion. Allow the plaster to firm up for a minute or two.

8. Starting on the top outside area of the moon, carve a row of mosaics, following the contour of the moon. Complete a single row around the moon perimeter before starting a second row.

9. Start a second row of mosaics inside the first row. Continue adding rows in this manner until you reach the center of the moon. Allow the plaster to dry before continuing.

10. Use the wire tool to clean any excess plaster from the grout lines and complete the tile shapes.

11. Use the fine grit sandpaper to smooth any surface variations or imperfections. Since this mosaic will be covered with silver leaf, it should be as smooth as possible.

12. Brush a coat of silver leaf adhesive over the plaster mosaic. Allow it to dry. Because the plaster is porous, apply a second coat of adhesive.

13. After the adhesive has had a chance to tack up, carefully transfer a sheet of silver leaf using a soft brush. Gently tap down the silver leaf with the mop brush to adhere the leaf to the surface.

14. Continue placing the silver leaf over the exposed sections of mosaic, until the entire area is covered.

15. Gently brush the silver leaf with your mop brush, pushing the silver in different directions.

16. Use the chisel brush to tap the silver into the grout joints. Don't worry if the leaf cracks within the joints, it adds to the unique look of the mosaic.

17. Spray two coats of sealer over the entire moon, allowing the coats to dry between applications. Matte sealer tends to give the silver an antique appearance, while gloss sealer retains the high metallic sheen.

18. Apply the metal leaf overlay. See next page.

Applying Metal Leaf Overlay

1. Prime the plaster mosaic with at least two coats of metal leaf adhesive. Allow the adhesive to dry clear before continuing to the next step.

2. Gently transfer a single sheet of silver leaf over the surface. Use a large soft brush to gently tap the silver leaf to the surface.

3. Use your brush to push the leaf down, brushing in different directions.

4. Bring your brush to the edge to hold down the leaf, and gently tear the excess away from the edge.

5. Once the edges are torn away, use a chisel brush, which is stiffer, to push the silver leaf into the spaces between the mosaic pieces.

The Sun

1. Seal the wood with a water-based sealer. Sand the surface after the first coat has dried, and apply a second coat.

2. Paint the sun with two coats of Metallic Copper to ensure good coverage. Allow it to dry completely before moving to the next step. This is the base coat for this project.

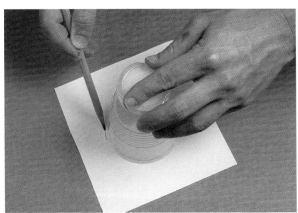

3. Place the circle template or glass on the paper and trace a circle. Remember to keep a ½" border around the circle.

4. Cut out the circle.

▲5. Spray one side of the leftover paper with spray stencil adhesive. Center the template on the sun, and press the circle edges down. Make sure the inside edges are pressed down firmly.

6. For the top coat, mix ¼ cup of plaster compound with ¼ teaspoon of Barnyard Red paint until the color is well blended.

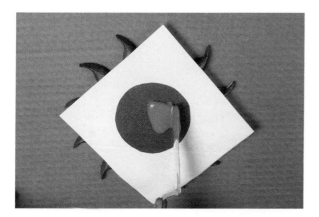 

▲7. Use the small palette knife to spread a ⅛" top coat over the center of the sun, spreading it slightly over the edges of the template. Move the palette knife in different directions to create some surface texture.

▲8. Immediately lift up the template from the surface. Allow the plaster to sit for a minute or two before proceeding.

9. Use the wire tool to carve out random grout joints.

10. Allow the plaster to dry completely. Don't sand the surface. Allow the texture to remain on the plaster.

11. Paint the mosaic pieces with two coats of Metallic Copper.

12. Use the liner brush to paint the grout joints Barnyard Red.

13. Spray two coats of sealer, allowing the coats to dry between applications.

Butterfly Coat Rack

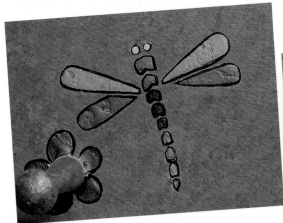

Butterfly Coat Rack

Functional, simple, and easy to create, this coat rack is at home in any child's bedroom. Adorned with a simple butterfly and dragonfly, it's ideal for a little girl or baby's room. Add a train or jungle animal, and you now have the perfect addition to a little boy's domain.

This project was created with custom-cut stencils. Cutting stencils is easy and gives you unlimited design possibilities. Your work area will need a heat-resistant surface. The stencil cutter uses heat to melt through the plastic stencil blank. Remember to keep this tool out of reach of children. It stays hot for a period of time after it's been unplugged.

▼ **YOU WILL NEED**
- Pegboard or hat rack*
- Plaster compound
- Artist's paint: Light Blue, Licorice, Metallic Rose Pearl, Metallic Blue Topaz, Metallic Christmas Green, Metallic Peridot, Metallic Amethyst, Wicker White, True Blue*
- Glaze: Cerulean*
- Matte or gloss sealer*
- Water-based wood sealer
- Stencil blank*
- Stencil cutter
- Stencil spray adhesive*
- Brushes: liner, filbert*
- 2" wide disposable brush
- Mopping tool
- Pallet knife*
- Medium and fine grit sandpaper
- Permanent marker
- Masking tape
- Disposable cups
- Paper plates

*Used in this project: Plaid paint, glaze, sealer, stencil blank, spray adhesive; Walnut Hollow hat rack; Dynasty Brushes; Kemper pallet knife.

Refer to page 30 for Stencil Cutting tips.

1. Seal the wood with a water-based sealer. Sand the surface after the first coat has dried, and apply a second coat.

2. Paint the hat rack with True Blue paint, allow it to dry, and apply a second coat to ensure good coverage.

3. Pour a small pool of Cerulean glaze onto a paper plate. Before using the mopping tool, dampen it with water and wring out any excess. Dip the mopping tool in the glaze, and dab it on a clean paper plate to remove the excess. Quickly dab the mopping tool to the surface, using a random pattern. Twisting your wrist as you go, will keep the pattern from repeating itself. Because the glaze has a slower drying time, there's time to work the glaze evenly onto the surface.

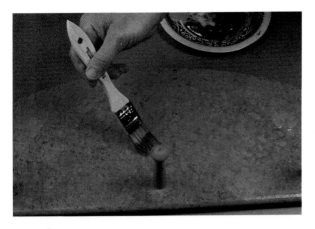

▲ **4.** Wait until the glaze becomes tacky, and then use the disposable brush to gently dry brush the surface in different directions. This will soften the mopping pattern. As the brush picks up glaze, wipe it dry on a paper towel before continuing.

5. Allow the rack to completely dry before proceeding.

6. Copy the butterfly, dragonfly, and daisy patterns from page 49 onto a clean sheet of paper. Use masking tape to secure them to a smooth flat surface.

7. Use masking tape to secure the blank stencil over the pattern, and use a permanent marker to trace the designs. This is also the time to make any additions or personal touches to the designs.

8. Remove the traced stencil, and use masking tape to secure it to a heat-resistant surface. A large smooth floor tile makes an ideal cutting surface.

9. With smooth slow movements, retrace your designs and cut them out. If there are any jagged edges left on the stencil, lay it on your surface and use the stencil cutter to smooth them out.

10. Spray the back of the stencil with stencil adhesive, and set it aside to tack up.

11. While the adhesive is tacking up, mix 2 tablespoons of plaster compound with ½ teaspoon of True Blue paint until the color is well blended.

▲ **12.** Position the dragonfly part of the stencil on the painted rack. Keeping the dragonfly at an angle is a more natural position than straight up and down.

13. Use the pallet knife to gently spread a ⅛" layer of plaster over the dragonfly stencil. Make sure the plaster barely covers the edges of the stencil, so as the stencil is pulled up, the edge is clean.

 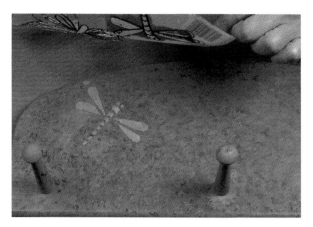

14. Firmly hold down one end of the stencil, and immediately pull up the opposite corner. Gently pull back until the stencil is completely removed. This keeps the stencil from shifting while it is being removed. Don't worry about peaks or sharp edges. These will be sanded down before the paint is applied.

15. Cut the daisy from the stencil, leaving a 1" border on all sides. Make one cut from the edge of the stencil to the edge of the design. Lightly spray the back with stencil adhesive, and allow the adhesive to tack up.

 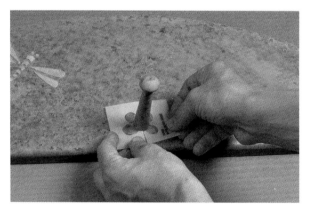

16. Pull the stencil apart, and gently twist it so the edges open enough to slide the stencil over the peg. Firmly push the stencil down once it is placed at the base of the peg. If it does not lay flat, remove it and trim off any excess stencil until it fits without bunching up.

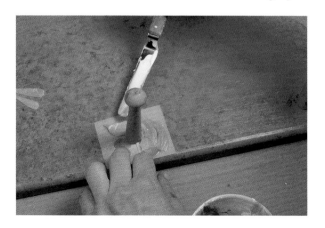

17. Apply the plaster compound over the daisy stencil, working around the peg. Avoid getting excessive plaster on the peg. If this happens, use a damp sponge to wipe it off before it firms up.

▲ **18.** Immediately lift and pull apart the stencil to remove it from the peg.

19. Because this stencil is used multiple times, remove the excess plaster from the stencil after each use. Apply the flower stencil to the remaining pegs, following steps 16–18.

20. Turn the stencil, and position the butterfly on the wood. Apply the butterfly in the same way as the dragonfly.

21. Allow the plaster to dry completely before continuing to the next step.

22. Once the plaster has dried, use medium grit sandpaper to smooth out any ridges, lumps, or surface inconsistencies. Be careful when sanding. Plaster is very soft, and aggressive sanding will sand the relief off. To sand more evenly, wrap the sandpaper around a small block of wood.

23. Use a filbert brush to paint the metallic colors on the butterfly, dragonfly, and daisy.

24. Once the paint has dried, use a liner brush to outline the elements with Licorice paint. Add any other painted elements, like antennae.

25. Use Wicker White paint between the butterfly pieces, or allow the background color to show, like the dragonfly.

26. To represent the centers of the daisy, dab Metallic Yellow paint to the pegs.

27. Once the project has completely dried, seal with a matte or gloss sealer.

Mosaic Box

Mosaic Box

Papier-mâché boxes are inexpensive and extremely versatile. They come in a variety of shapes and sizes, and they're adaptable to a wide range of decorative treatments. This box is the perfect size for toiletries, cotton balls, keepsakes, or for display.

For ease of application, the top is done in two parts. This allows you to handle the top without spoiling the work you have just completed. The base can be painted using any decorative technique, but the crackle finish works well with the aged appearance of the mosaic top. Remember, because this box has a top and a bottom, you can expedite the process by working on one half while the other half is drying.

▼ **YOU WILL NEED**
- 4" papier-mâché box
- Plaster compound
- Artist's pigment: Pure Black, Raw Sienna*
- Artist's paint: Licorice, Barnyard Red*
- Crackle medium*
- Matte sealer*
- Brushes: liner, filbert, flat brush*
- Wire tool*
- Putty or palette knife
- Fine sandpaper
- Waxed paper
- Plastic wrap

*Used in this project: Plaid pigment, paint, crackle medium, sealer; Kemper wire tool; Dynasty brushes.

Review General Instructions, page 18, before beginning this project.

1. For the base coat, mix 2 tablespoons of plaster compound with ½ teaspoon of Black artist's pigment, until the color is well blended.

2. Use the putty knife to spread a ⅛" base coat evenly over the top and sides of the papier-mâché box top, as if frosting a cake. Don't worry about jagged edges or bumps. Those can be sanded off after the plaster has dried.

3. While the top is drying, base coat the bottom of the box with Licorice paint. Apply two thin coats rather than one thick coat. The first thin coat will dry quickly, sealing the box from the moisture in later coats. One thick coat of paint may cause bubbles or warping.

4. When your box top has completely dried, the color will lighten up a shade or two. Use fine sandpaper to gently sand the edges. It's best to do this outside or in a well-ventilated area. Sand until the surface is smooth. Don't sand too hard, or you'll sand through the outer surface. This base coat will act as the grout line between the mosaic pieces.

5. Once the top has been sanded, it's time to mix the plaster that will represent the mosaic pieces. Mix two tablespoons of plaster compound and ¼ teaspoon of Raw Sienna. Blend the color until there are no streaks or lumps. It should be ivory or bone color.

6. The top of the box is done in two steps to allow for easy handling. The top surface will be done first and allowed to dry to the touch. Then the sides will be done. Cover the plaster compound with plastic wrap between stages, so it will not dry out. Use the putty knife to spread ⅛" layer of Raw Sienna plaster compound over the top of the box top. Let dry for a minute or two until the top is dry to the touch. Save the remaining plaster compound for the sides of the box top.

7. Lay a piece of waxed paper over the pattern provided on page 53. Tape down the corners to keep the waxed paper in place.

8. With a liner brush, trace over the pattern with Black paint. Apply the paint heavily, and move quickly so the paint will be wet enough to transfer to the top.

9. Line up the design with the top of the box, and gently lay the waxed paper, paint side down, on the surface. Lightly run you fingers over the lines, and then quickly peel away the waxed paper. The transfer does not have to be perfect. Mistakes can easily be corrected.

10. Use a filbert brush to gently paint the design. Because you're painting on wet plaster, strokes must be gentle, and the paint needs to flow over the surface. You will quickly discover that any mistakes are easy to fix.

11. With the wire tool, start carving from left to right or from top to bottom. Outline the painted design, and then carve out the pieces. After one section of the design is carved, carve out the background pieces before moving to the next portion. After the entire top has been carved, allow it to dry.

12. While the top of the box is drying, you can finish the decorative painting on the bottom portion. Once the base coat has dried, apply the crackle medium. The key to a good crackle technique is applying the medium evenly and without overlapping strokes. Following the manufacturer's guidelines, allow the medium to dry until it's slightly tacky.

13. With a flat brush, paint Barnyard Red over the crackle medium. Paint in various directions to vary the crackle effect. Avoid overlapping brush strokes, which will effect the crackling development. Allow it to dry, and seal the base of the box with a light coat of matte sealer.

14. Once the box top is dry to the touch, proceed with the box top sides. Use the Raw Sienna plaster that was saved from the box top and apply a ⅛" coat of plaster to the sides of the box top. Any ridges can be sanded after it's dried.

15. Allow the plaster to sit for a minute or two to firm up. Using the wire tool, carve a simple mosaic pattern along the sides. Don't worry about painting your Black edge. That will be done after the top has dried.

16. Once the top has completely dried, use the wire tool to go over your mosaic pattern, cleaning out any plaster that might be caught between the pieces.

17. Use fine sandpaper to lightly sand the top edge and ridges that remain.

18. With a liner brush, paint the mosaic pieces that run along the edge of the top with Black.

19. Using the same liner brush used for the box top sides, paint over the design where the sandpaper might have taken off any of the color. Use Barnyard Red to go over the design where the color might have been sanded off.

20. Once the project has completely dried, seal with matte sealer.

tip ▶ **C**rackle finishes can be frustrating when they don't come out the way you had hoped. There are a few basic rules to remember to achieve good results every time.

- Allow your base coat to completely dry before applying your crackle medium.
- Apply your crackle medium with a soft brush, keeping in mind that the amount of medium will effect the size of the cracks.
- When applying your top coat, brush in one direction, trying not to overlap your brush strokes.

tip ▶ **I**f you are planning to do multiple projects or a large project, apply your base coat the day before, so you can get started without the wait.

Tissue Box

Tissue Box

The tissue box is one accessory that we can never do without, and it's also one we least like to exhibit. Now you can create a tissue box holder that will not only match your decor, but it will resemble a piece of art.

This tissue box was created using pearlizing medium for a mother-of-pearl effect. Pastel shades were used for the grout and top coat, rather than the usual black and white.

▼ YOU WILL NEED

- Wood tissue box holder
- Plaster compound
- Artist's pigment: Permanent Rose, Yellow Light*
- Artist's paint: Metallic Champagne, Taupe, Sahara Gold, Inca Gold, Antique Copper*
- Pearlizing medium
- Matte sealer
- Wire tool*
- Brushes: filbert or chisel brush*
- Putty knife
- Medium and fine grit sandpaper
- Small block of wood, 1" x 2"

*Used in this project: Plaid paints and pigments; Kemper wire tools; Dynasty brushes.

Review General Instructions, page 18, before beginning this project.

1. Seal the wood using a water-based sealer. Sand the surface with fine grit sandpaper after the first coat has dried, and apply a second coat.

2. For the base coat, mix 1 cup of plaster compound with 1 teaspoon of Permanent Rose pigment until the color is well blended.

3. Use the putty knife to spread a ⅛" base coat over the top of the tissue holder and two of the sides. Depending on the size of your tissue box, you may want to use a larger putty knife. The larger the putty knife, the easier it is to spread an even smooth coat of plaster. Cover your remaining plaster with plastic wrap for later use, and allow the tissue holder to dry completely.

4. Continue by applying the plaster to the remaining two sides. Allow them to dry completely.

5. Use the medium grit sandpaper over a small block of wood to sand the sides smooth and flat. Clean off the edges to keep the corners square and sharp.

6. For the top coat, mix 1 cup of plaster with ½ teaspoon of Yellow Light pigment until the color is well blended.

7. Working two sides at a time, apply the top coat to the top of the tissue box and one side, keeping the layer as smooth as possible.

8. Allow the plaster to firm up for a minute, and transfer the small fish and shell designs in a random pattern.

9. Use the wire tool to quickly carve out the design. Allow the plaster to dry.

10. Repeat steps 6–9 for the remaining sides.

11. After all of the sides have been completely covered and carved, use the wire tool to clean out the grout joint, complete tile shapes, and alter the design.

12. Use the fine grit sandpaper over a small block of wood to sand the sides smooth and flat. Pay special attention to edges and corners.

13. Paint in the shells. Use the pearlizing medium to paint random background pieces.

14. Seal with a matte sealer.

Flowerpot

Flower Pot

The obvious choice for a mosaic is a terra cotta flowerpot. If this pot is going to be placed inside with a silk plant or in a setting where water is not a factor, then the pot does not need to be pretreated. If this pot is going to be used with a real plant indoors, then the interior of the pot will need to be treated with a water-barrier spray. There are various waterproofing mediums on the market. If the pot is going to be used outside, then an exterior plaster compound will need to be used. And once it's dried, it will need to be treated with an exterior varnish.

To simplify the process, the pot shown here will be an indoor pot without the real plant. You could use the pot for a topiary decoration or as a place to store utensils, pencils, or odds and ends.

▼ YOU WILL NEED

- Terra cotta pot (8" pot used here)
- Plaster compound
- Artist's paint: Licorice, Thicket, Italian Sage, Peridot, Warm White*
- Wire tool*
- Brushes: small chisel brush*
- Medium putty knife
- Medium and fine grit sandpaper
- Optional: turntable* OR small board or sturdy piece of card board

*Used in this project: Plaid paint; Kemper wire tool, turntable; Dynasty brushes.

Review General Instructions, page 18, before beginning this project.

1. For the base coat, mix 1 cup of plaster compound with ½ tablespoon Licorice paint until the color is well blended.

 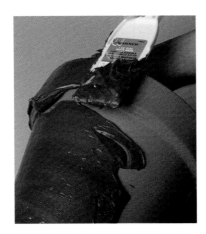 

2. Turn the pot upside down, and hold it on your fist. With your other hand, spread a generous base coat onto the pot, like you would ice a cake. Make sure to follow the contours of the pot, including the rim.

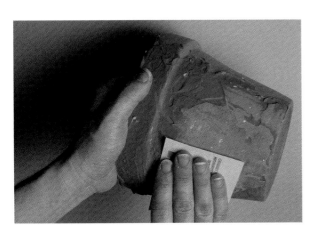

3. Allow the pot to completely dry. Use the medium grit sandpaper to sand around the pot, keeping the round contours. Curving your hand around the pot as you sand will result in a smooth rounded surface. Don't sand too hard, or the pot will show through.

4. For the top coat, mix 1 cup of plaster with ½ teaspoon Warm White paint until the color is well blended.

5. Apply a ⅛" top coat, keeping to the contours of the pot. Allow the surface to firm up before proceeding.

6. Transfer the design onto the pot, and place it on the turntable or a small piece of board. Using the turntable or board will allow you to turn the flowerpot without touching the pot.

tip

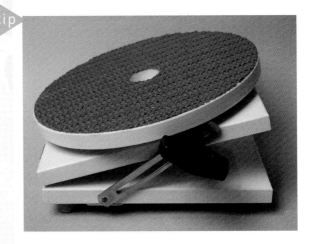

This turntable by Kemper allows you to turn your project smoothly and keeps your hands free.

7. Work quickly with a small wire loop to carve out the design. Allow the surface to completely dry before proceeding.

8. Use the wire tool to clean out the grout joints, remove excess plaster, and take out a few tiles to give it an authentic mosaic look.

9. Use the fine grit sandpaper to clean up the edges and smooth out the surface.

10. Because sanding the surface may have taken off some of the color, use the small chisel brush to touch up the colors. This is a great time to change colors or add details, as desired.

11. Seal with a satin gloss varnish.

tip **R**emember that if this piece is going outside, it will need numerous coats of varnish, which will have to be reapplied periodically.

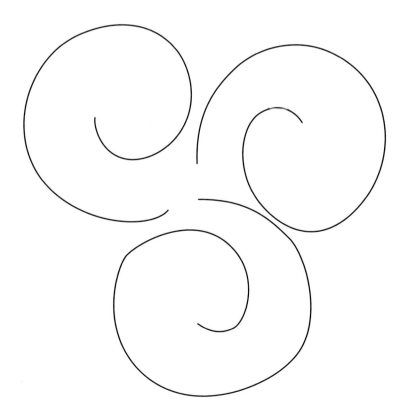

Wall Clock

Wall Clock

This wall clock was inspired by mosaics made from broken china plates. The edges of the mosaic are rounded, and the design is reminiscent of a rose china pattern. Notice that the colors are blended rather than each piece being made up of a solid color. This visually allows the pieces to work together, creating the rose image.

▼ YOU WILL NEED

- Wood clock plaque*
- Clock mechanisms, including clock number decal*
- Plaster compound
- Artist's pigment: Titanium White*
- Artist's paint: Spring Rose, Rose Garden, Berry Wine, Old Ivy, Hunter Green*
- Clear acrylic spray
- Wire tool*
- Brushes: filbert*
- Sponge brush
- Large putty knife
- Medium and fine grit sandpaper

*Used in this project: Walnut Hollow clock plaque, clock mechanism; Plaid pigments, paint; Kemper wire tool; Dynasty brushes.

Review General Instructions, page 18, before beginning this project.

1. Make four copies of the rose design, page 65.

2. Seal the clock plaque with two coats of water-based sealer, sanding between coats.

3. Use the sponge brush to paint two coats of Titanium White pigment to ensure good coverage.

▲4. Cut around the number decal, and peel the backing off. The number decal will have a hole in the center, where the clock mechanism will go through. Place the numbers on the edge of a clean surface for later use. The backing will be used as a stencil for the center of the clock. Spray the number backing with a very light mist of stencil adhesive, and allow it to dry.

▲5. The clock plaque will have a hole, where the clock mechanism will go through. Line up the stencil, made from number backing, with the hole that is in the center of the clock plaque.

6. For the base coat, mix 1 cup of plaster compound with 1 tablespoon of Titanium White pigment until the color is well blended.

▲7. Use the large putty knife to spread an even layer of plaster over the surface, rounding the corners. Spread the plaster towards the center of the clock, barely covering the edges of the number stencil.

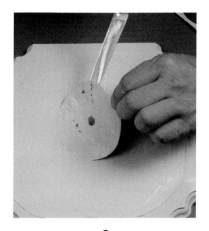 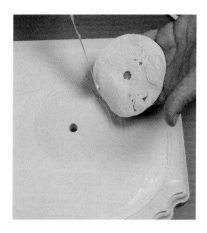 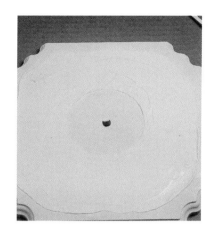

▲ **8.** Use a knife or wire tool to gently peel up an edge and then pull it completely off the face of the plaque. Allow the base coat to dry before proceeding.

9. Use the medium grit sandpaper to sand the surface smooth.

10. For the top coat, mix 1 cup of plaster to ½ teaspoon of Spring Rose paint until the colors are well blended.

◄ **11.** Use the putty knife to spread a very thin layer of the Spring Rose plaster over the base coat, thinning the layer out as you move to the edges.

12. Once the plaster has firmed up for a minute or two, transfer the design to the front of the clock using one of the transfer methods discussed in the General Instructions. Center a rose on each side of the clock, with the leaves touching.

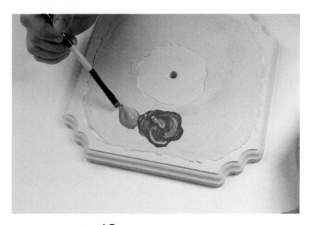 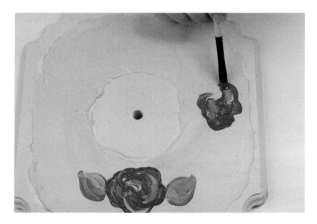

▲ **13.** Quickly paint in the roses. Allow the colors to blend and swirl with each other.

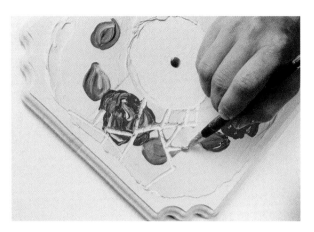

▲ **14.** Use the wire tool to make random tile cuts. Keep the pieces in a shard shape to mimic broken china.

15. Round off the corners to give the mosaic a plate shape. Allow the mosaic to completely dry before continuing.

16. Use the wire tool to clean out the plaster from the grout joints, the circle for the number decal, and the rounded corners.

17. Use the fine grit sandpaper to smooth out any ridges or bumps.

18. Once the surface is smooth, touch up the flowers and leaves, allowing the colors to blend with each other.

19. Spray the surface with two or more coats of clear acrylic sealer.

20. Take the clock numbers, and carefully center them in the middle of the clock, lining up the holes.

21. Attach the clock mechanism to the plaque, according to the manufacturer's directions.

Triangle Flag Box

Triangle Flag Box

Not everything turns into a project idea until you actually hold the items in your hands. This Flag Box was not a planned project until I held the box. Maybe the idea came as a result of the turmoil this country and its people have felt recently. I'm not sure. But the moment I held this box, the image of a folded flag came to mind. The image in my mind is much more serious than the actual project. This box is fun and playful, but still retains the dignity of the flag it represents.

▼ YOU WILL NEED

- Triangle-shaped wood box*
- Plaster compound
- Artist's pigment: Pure Black, Indian Blue, Napthol Crimson*
- Artist's paint: Lipstick Red, Brilliant Blue, Wicker White, Licorice*
- Water-based wood sealer
- High gloss varnish
- Wire tool*
- Brushes: chiseled brush (small and large)*
- Palette knife*
- Large putty knife
- Medium and fine grit sandpaper
- ½" Painter's tape or masking tape

*Used in this project: Walnut Hollow triangle box; Plaid paint, pigment; Kemper wire tool, palette knife; Dynasty brushes.

Review General Instructions, page 18, before beginning this project.

1. Seal the wood using a water-based sealer. Use the fine grit sandpaper to sand the surface after the first coat has dried. Apply a second coat.

2. Paint the sides of the box with Wicker White and allow them to dry. Apply a second coat to ensure good coverage. The white will be the white stripes on the box.

3. Apply two coats of Licorice paint to the top of the box, allowing the paint to dry between coats. Avoid getting black paint on the sides of the box. It helps to brush the paint with outward strokes, letting the brush move over the top edges.

▲ **4.** Apply three rows of masking tape horizontally around the sides of the box. The distance between the rows of masking tape should be the approximate width of the tape itself. These will represent the white and red stripes of the flag. Because there are hinges on the back side of the box, tape the two front sides, and allow the back to remain white.

5. Mix 3 tablespoons of plaster compound with ½ teaspoon of Napthol Crimson until the color is well blended.

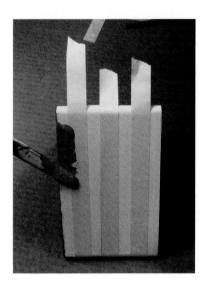 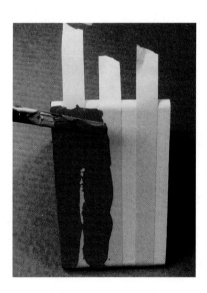 

▲ **6.** Use a putty knife to apply the crimson plaster to the areas between the tape, keeping the thickness consistent.

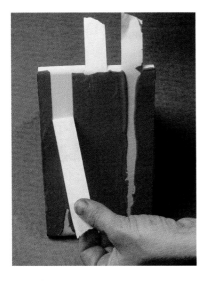 

△7. Immediately remove the tape by pulling straight up and away from the box.

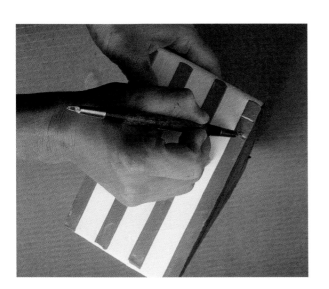 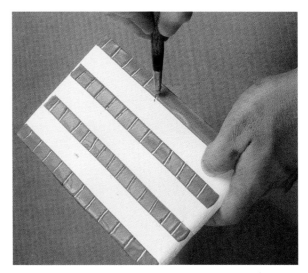

△8. Allow the crimson stripes to become slightly firm, and then use a wire tool to quickly carve straight vertical grout lines across the crimson stripes. These tiles should be consistent and square.

9. Allow the crimson stripes to dry, and then sand with fine grit sandpaper.

10. Mix ½ teaspoon of Licorice paint with 1 cup of plaster until the color is well blended.

11. Apply the Licorice plaster to the top of the box with a palette knife. Allow it to dry, and then sand it before proceeding to the next step.

▲ **12.** Mix two tablespoons of plaster with ½ teaspoon of Indian Blue until the color is well blended. Apply the blue plaster to the box top with a large putty knife.

13. Allow the plaster to firm slightly and transfer the first star to the center of the box top. Continue to place the stars in an evenly spaced pattern, working around the first star. Make sure some of the stars continue off the top of the box to keep the pattern flowing.

14. After the stars are carved out, continue to carve out the background area, making the pieces triangular in shape. This will mimic the shape of the box as well as the basic shapes that make up the stars.

15. Allow the top to completely dry, and then sand with fine grit sandpaper.

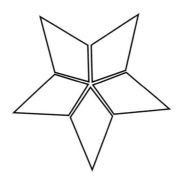

16. Use a small chisel brush to paint the stars Wicker White. The brush allows you to paint the tips of the stars, while keeping the paint on top of the plaster and not in the grout joint.

17. Since the plaster already appears light blue, paint every other piece with Brilliant Blue.

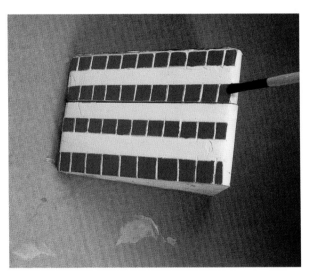

18. With the small chisel brush, paint the red stripe pieces over with Lipstick Red. This will intensify the color and give you a truer red.

19. Touch up the paint on the white strips.

20. Allow the box to dry, and seal with a high gloss varnish.

Picture Frame

Picture Frame

I always say, "what is there that hasn't been made into a picture frame?" Not only can you take just about anything and make it into a frame, but if you don't have a picture you can put a mirror in the frame.

This wood frame is unique for a number of reasons: One, it's very natural with the bark still attached to the frame. Two, the shape is asymmetrical, while the picture opening is perfectly rectangular. This offsets the picture, giving it loads of interest. And three, we will treat it with a very non-traditional mosaic look. The leaves are overlapped and cascading in one direction. The image of leaves works well with the bark and the organic shape. It's important not to be too caught up in the perfect leaf shape. Once you carve one, vary the shapes and position. This is a keepsake that will hold special meaning, once you fill it with a special picture.

▼ YOU WILL NEED

- Wood frame*
- Plaster compound
- Artist's pigment: Light Red Oxide, Yellow Ochre*
- Artist's paint: Licorice, Metallic Antique Copper, Metallic Inca Gold, Metallic Solid Bronze, Metallic Peridot*
- Water-based wood sealer
- High gloss varnish
- Wire tool*
- Brushes: filbert*
- Putty knife
- Fine and medium grit sandpaper
- Masking tape

*Used in this project: Walnut Hollow wood frame; Plaid paint, pigment; Kemper wire tool; Dynasty brush.

Review General Instructions, page 18, before beginning this project.

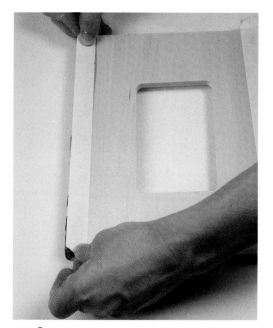

▲**1.** Seal the wood frame with one coat of wood sealer, and then apply a high gloss varnish to the bark.

▲**2.** Use masking tape to tape off both sides of the frame, covering the bark.

3. For the base coat, mix 2 tablespoons of plaster compound with ½ teaspoon of Light Red Oxide pigment and ¼ teaspoon of Licorice paint until the colors are well blended. To keep the color from becoming muddy, add small amounts of Licorice at a time.

◄**4.** Use the putty knife to spread an ⅛" base coat evenly over the frame. Spread the plaster over the edges of the tape and along the inside edges of the frame opening. Do not worry about jagged or uneven edges. These can be sanded off once the plaster has dried.

5. To pull the masking tape from the frame, push down on one end of the masking tape and immediately lift the top edge of the other end and pull it towards you. Allow the base coat to completely dry before moving on to the next step.

▲ **6.** Use medium grit sandpaper to sand the base coat smooth. Any rough edges along the frame opening should be sanded off a little at a time. Depending on the amount of plaster that was put on the frame opening, the edge can be sanded square or the opening can be slightly rounded to give a softer appearance.

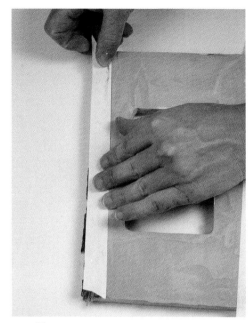

▲ **7.** Again, use masking tape to tape off both sides of the frame, covering the bark.

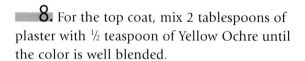
8. For the top coat, mix 2 tablespoons of plaster with ½ teaspoon of Yellow Ochre until the color is well blended.

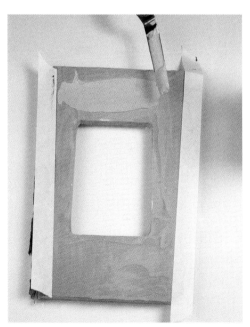

▲ **9.** Use the putty knife to spread a ⅛" top coat evenly over the frame front. Do not cover the inside frame opening. The color of the base coat will show on the finished project.

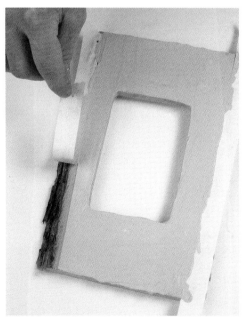

▲ **10.** Grasp the top of the tape, and immediately pull the masking tape from the frame.

▲**11.** Once the top coat has firmed up, use the wire tool to carve out leaves in a random pattern. Keep the leaves running in the same direction. It is easier to carve out whole leaves randomly around the frame, and then fill in with partial leaves.

12. Allow the top coat to dry, and use fine grit sandpaper to sand the surface smooth. Then use the wire tool to clean out any grout joints or finish any leaf shapes.

13. Paint the leaves in various metallic shades.

▲**14.** Seal the entire surface, including the bark, with a high gloss varnish. Apply two coats for maximum shine and durability.

tip ▶ Practice your leaves by drawing them freehand on a piece of paper before you begin the project.

House Numbers

House Numbers

Although house numbers are a necessity, there's no reason that they can't reflect your more artistic side. These numbers are placed on individual wood plaques, which can be painted different colors. Or, you can place all of the numbers on one large plaque.

I recommend that you hang these house numbers in a protected area, like under a porch. But not to worry, the bright Santa Fe colors should be noticeable from a distance.

▼ YOU WILL NEED
- 5" x 5" wood plaque
- Plaster compound
- Artist's pigment: Cobalt*
- Artist's paint: Autumn Leaves, Wicker White, Metallic Copper*
- Water-based wood sealer
- Wire tool*
- Brushes: chisel*
- Small palette knife
- Medium sandpaper
- Masking tape
- Scissors

*Used in this project: Plaid pigments, paints; Kemper wire tool; Dynasty brushes.

Review General Instructions, page 18, before beginning this project.

1. Seal the wood with a water-based sealer. Sand and apply a second coat.

2. Paint a 1½" border, including the sides, with Cobalt.

3. Allow it to dry, sand, and apply a second coat. Sanding between coats of paint will give you a smooth painted surface, while the second coat intensifies the color.

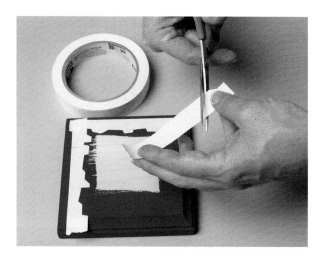

4. After the paint has dried, cut four 5" pieces of masking tape. Cut random shapes out of one side of the tape. There's no need to plan how the tape will be cut because a random pattern is part of the charm.

5. Line up the straight side of the tape with the edge of the plaque, and firmly press down. Remember that the inside edge is important. If it does not adhere well to the surface, plaster could creep under the edge.

6. Apply the other three pieces on the remaining sides.

7. For the base coat, mix 1 tablespoon of plaster compound with 1/4 teaspoon of Autumn Leaves paint until the color is well blended.

8. Use the small palette knife to smooth a very thin layer of the base coat on the center of the plaque, slightly overlapping the taped edge.

9. Smooth out the plaster until it barely covers the tape.

▲ **10.** In a clean upward motion, immediately pull the tape off of all four sides. Pull the tape in the order that it was applied, so the piece you are removing will not pull up other pieces.

▲ **11.** After the tape is removed, allow the base coat to completely dry.

12. Sand the surface smooth with the medium grit sandpaper.

13. For the top coat, mix another tablespoon of plaster with ¼ teaspoon of Autumn Leaves paint until the color is well blended.

14. Use the small palette knife to carefully smooth a thin layer of top coat over the base coat. Follow the shape of the base coat, leaving a thin border.

15. Allow the plaster to firm up slightly, and then transfer the number pattern to the center of your plaster coating. Because this is a small project, it would also be easy to freehand your numbers. Practice your style on a separate sheet of paper. If this is an address with many numbers, it is important that each one be done in the same style.

16. Use the wire tool to carve out the number, using consistent shapes. Then carve out the background in random shapes and sizes. Allow the plaster to dry.

17. Use the wire tool to clean out the grout joints.

▲18. Lightly sand the surface to remove the jagged plaster pieces, but allow some of the texture that was created during the application to show.

▲19. Use a chisel brush to paint the number with Wicker White and the background with Metallic Copper.

▲20. Seal the project with three or more coats of clear acrylic spray. Every coat of clear acrylic adds shine and protects the mosaic.

tip▶ Acrylic spray provides a clear smooth surface if it is applied correctly. Always keep in mind that two light coats are much better than one heavy coat. Hold the can 10" from your surface, and with a sideways sweeping motion, spray your surface keeping the can moving and slightly overlapping each stroke. Allow the first coat to dry before applying a second coat. Remember that the higher the humidity, the slower the acrylic spray will dry.

1 2 3 4 5 6 7 8 9 0

Serving Tray

Serving Tray

This project is very versatile. It can be hung on the wall as a piece of art, or it can be used as a functional serving tray. To use it as a serving tray, place a piece of glass over the mosaic to protect it.

A dramatic finish was used to frame this classic design. Gold leafing has enjoyed a welcome resurgence in popularity the past few years. Luckily with innovations in the craft industry, a gold leaf look-alike is available at a fraction of the cost of the real thing.

▼ YOU WILL NEED

- 12" x 12" wood serving tray*
- Artist's canvas board (Larger than 12" x 12")
- Plaster compound
- Artist's paint: Barnyard Red, Terra Cotta, True Burgundy, Cappuccino, Peach Cobbler, Licorice, Dark Brown, Fawn*
- Gold leafing kit
- Water-based wood sealer
- Matte or satin varnish
- Wire tool*
- Brushes: large and small chisel brush*
- Large putty knife
- Medium and fine grit sandpaper
- Contact cement

*Used in this project: Plaid wooden tray, pigments, paints; Kemper wire tools; Dynasty brushes.

Review General Instructions, page 18, before beginning this project.

1. Seal the wooden tray with two coats of wood sealer, sanding lightly between coats with fine grit sandpaper.

2. Cut the artist's canvas board to fit the interior of the tray, using a straight edge and a sharp blade to score the board a few times to cut through the backing. Bend the board and cut through the canvas weave on the front of the board.

3. For the base coat, mix 1 cup of plaster compound with 1 teaspoon of Licorice paint until the color is well blended.

4. Use the large putty knife to spread a ⅛" layer of plaster over the surface of the canvas board. Set it aside to dry.

5. While the plaster is drying, use the large chisel brush to paint the sides of the tray, both inside and out, and the top rim with two coats of Barnyard Red. Allow it to completely dry before proceeding.

6. Once the base coat has dried on the board, sand the surface with the medium grit sandpaper, smoothing out any large ridges or lumps.

7. Apply a generous coating of gold leaf adhesive to the areas painted Barnyard Red. Allow the adhesive it to dry until it becomes tacky, or according to the manufacturer's suggestions.

8. Apply the gold leaf in sections. Lay it down, rub your fingers over it, and quickly pull up, depositing the gold leaf.

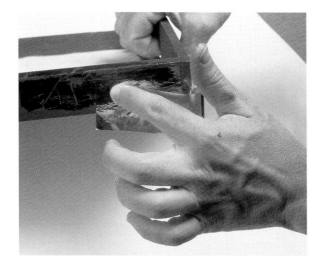

9. Once the gold leaf is pulled off, you can reapply the leaf again and again, filling in any bare areas.

10. Once the gold leaf is on, spray the surface with a clear acrylic sealer.

11. For the top coat, mix 1 cup of plaster with ½ teaspoon of Fawn paint until the color is well blended.

12. Use the large putty knife to smooth a thin layer of the top coat over the base coat on the canvas board. Working with full smooth strokes will help keep the layer consistent and smooth.

13. Allow the top coat to firm, and transfer the design.

14. Using quick strokes, paint in large portions of the design in a blocky fashion. Remember, these colors will be divided when they are carved into mosaics.

15. Use the wire tool to carve out sections, starting at the right top corner. Move across and down the picture, always carving out the focus area first, like the woman, and then working on the background.

16. Completely carve out pieces of mosaic throughout to give it an aged appearance. Allow the mosaic to dry.

17. Use the wire tool to clean out the grout joints and complete any unfinished pieces.

18. Use the fine sandpaper to smooth out any ridges or bumps. If an aged look is desired, sand the surface lightly in a circular motion to take off paint in areas. Sanding in a circular motion allows the paint to appear faded rather than purposely taken off.

19. Use the chisel brush to touch up areas with their original colors.

20. Seal the mosaic with a clear matte or satin varnish.

21. Secure the mosaic in the bottom of the tray using contact cement. If the edges are not cut perfect, use small pieces of wood trim to cover any imperfections in the fit. The tray can be hung up on the wall like a picture. Or, once glass is placed over the surface, it may be used as a functional tray.

Enlarge this pattern 150%.

Mosaic Birdhouse

Mosaic Birdhouse

What's more charming than a birdhouse, whether it's in the garden or on a fireplace mantel? This birdhouse incorporates all the charm of broken faux blue and white china mosaics with a thatched moss roof. Although it looks difficult, it's not only easy, but it's also very quick.

The variation to this project is in the type of plaster compound that's used. This birdhouse was made with interior plaster compound, but you can use exterior plaster and place the birdhouse in a protected outside location. Remember to seal it well with a few coats of gloss sealer. The gloss sealer helps create the illusion of broken china dishes.

▼ YOU WILL NEED
- Wood birdhouse*
- Plaster compound
- Artist's paint: Wicker White, Brilliant Blue, Clover*
- Natural moss
- Water-based wood sealer
- Gloss sealer
- Wire tool*
- Brushes: liner*
- Small putty knife
- Fine and medium grit sandpaper

*Used in this project: Plaid paint; Kemper wire tool; Dynasty brushes; Walnut Hollow birdhouse.

Review General Instructions, page 18, before beginning this project.

1. Seal the wood with a water-based sealer. Sand the surface after the first coat has dried, and then apply a second coat.

2. Paint the birdhouse with Wicker White. Apply a second coat to ensure good coverage.

3. For the basecoat, mix 1 cup of plaster compound with two tablespoons of Wicker White paint until the color is well blended. This will be your white grout joint.

tip The plaster compound used in the blue and white birdhouse was interior grade. To use this piece in a sheltered outside area, it must be made with exterior plaster compound.

4. Use the putty knife to spread a ⅛" layer of the Wicker White plaster evenly over all four sides of the birdhouse. Allow it to completely dry before proceeding to the next step.

5. Use the medium grit sandpaper to sand any jagged edges or inconsistencies.

6. For the top coat, mix another 1 cup of plaster compound with 1½ tablespoons of Wicker White paint until the color is well blended.

7. With a large putty knife, spread an even layer of the top coat over two sides of the birdhouse. Because the birdhouse will be handled, it is easier to complete two sides at a time. Cover the remaining plaster with plastic wrap. You will use it later on the other sides.

8. Once the top coat has firmed up, use the liner brush and Brilliant Blue to paint random swirls, leaves, or flowers. Keep the design flowing and random.

tip ▶ **T**his project mimics the look of broken blue and white china, so the pieces are carved in a shard pattern. The design is painted randomly, to imitate a flowery blue pattern, which was broken.

Carving all of tile sides on a corner or edge completes the illusion of china pieces.

▲**9.** After the design is complete, use the wire tool to carve out jagged tile pieces.

10. Allow it to dry. Repeat steps 7–9 for the remaining two sides.

11. After all four sides are dry, use the wire tool to go over your mosaic pattern, cleaning out any plaster that might be caught between the pieces.

12. Use fine sandpaper to lightly sand any jagged edges.

13. Touch up any areas with Brilliant Blue.

14. Paint the front edge of the roof, bird perch, and base with Clover.

15. Once the project has completely dried, seal with a gloss sealer.

16. Apply glue to the front edge of the roof, and to one side of the roof top.

17. Lay a sheet of green moss, starting at the ridge, and overhanging the front by ½ inch.

18. While firmly pressing down, fold the overhanging moss over the front edge.

19. Repeat on the other side of the roof top.

20. Attach a hook and eye through the ridge of the roof to hang the birdhouse, or display it on a shelf.

In this birdhouse variation, the plaster mosaic is used as an accent.

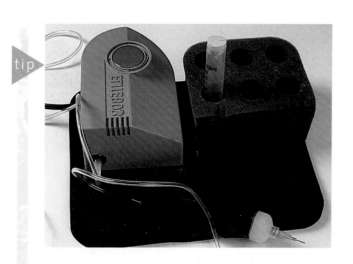

The Air Pen can be used to render very small and precise detail as shown in the birdhouse variation.

Marbleized Box

Marbleized Box

This box is a bundle of illusions and specialized painting techniques. It looks complicated, but it's actually very easy once the steps are broken down. The plaster compound used here is an example of what's used to build more structural elements than mosaics.

▼ **YOU WILL NEED**
- Footed wooden box
- Plaster compound
- Artist's paint: Licorice, Light Gray, Dark Gray, Wicker White*
- Artist's specialty products: acrylic extender, thickener
- Small feather
- Stencil blank
- Stencil cutter
- Stencil adhesive or tape
- "Prepared" small square sponge
- Water-based wood sealer
- High gloss varnish
- Sponge brush
- Small palette knife
- Medium and fine grit sandpaper
- Masking tape
- Paper plate

*Used in this project: Walnut Hollow box; Plaid paint, stencil, stencil cutter.

Review General Instructions, page 18, before beginning this project.

Review Mableizing, page 32.

1. Seal the wood using a water-based sealer. Sand the surface with fine grit sandpaper after the first coat has dried, and apply a second coat.

2. With the sponge brush, paint the lid, bottom edge, and ball feet with Licorice paint. Once the first coat has dried, sand with fine sandpaper, and apply a second coat.

3. Paint the four sides with Wicker White paint. Sand the surface, and apply a second coat to ensure good coverage.

4. Use your masking tape to tape off a ½"-wide border on all four sides of the box. You will be covering the area in the middle of the box and exposing the border around the edges of each side.

5. For the base coat, mix ½ cup of plaster compound with one tablespoon of Licorice paint until the color is well blended. Allow it to sit for a minute to firm up before proceeding.

6. Apply the mixture to the four edges of each side of the box, keeping the layer as smooth and consistent as possible.

7. Immediately peel the masking tape away from the edges, revealing a built-up border around the box edges. Allow the plaster to dry completely before proceeding to the next step.

8. Use the medium grit sandpaper to sand the edges as smooth as possible, keeping the corners of the box sharp.

9. Paint the plaster border with two coats of Licorice, allowing the first coat to dry before painting the second.

10. Starting with the areas that are Licorice, apply the marbleizing texture by sponging on your dark gray, extender, and thickener in a random pattern. Don't worry about the white areas. They can be touched up afterwards.

11. Use the feather to apply the light gray veining to the marbleized areas. Allow it to completely dry before proceeding.

12. Touch up any white areas before starting the white marble technique.

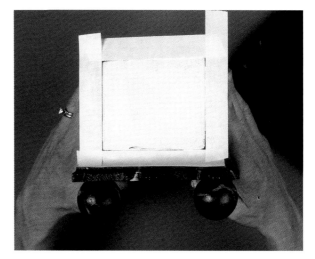

13. Tape off the black border.

14. Because the white area is so small, the sponge may be torn in half to allow for easier handling. Apply the Light Gray, Wicker White, extender, and thickener with a sponge to the four sides of the box using random presses. Applying the second coat, mixed with other colors, will give you color depth.

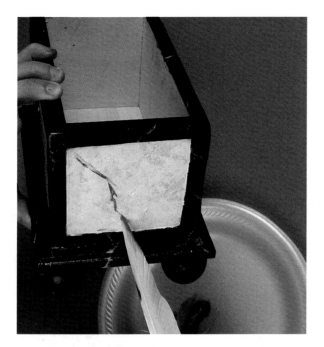 

▲ **15.** Use the feather to apply the dark gray veining to the white marbleized areas. Keep the marble veins running in the same direction. Allow the paint to completely dry before proceeding.

16. Use the pattern on page 98 to copy and cut out the stencil. See Stencil Cutting, page 30.

▲ **17.** Secure the blank stencil on the pattern, and then trace with a felt tip marker.

▲ **18.** Both the pattern and the stencil can be used over again.

19. For the relief design in the center of the box, mix 1 tablespoon of plaster to ½ teaspoon of Licorice paint until the colors are only slightly blended. This will give the appearance of a marbleized stone once the plaster is applied to the box.

20. Center the stencil in the middle of the long side of the box, using a stencil adhesive or tape to secure it in place.

21. With the small palette knife, spread a thin layer across the stencil.

22. Immediately lift the stencil by one corner, pulling up and across the surface.

23. Allow the stenciled plaster to completely dry, and sand it smooth with the fine grit sandpaper. Complete the other side.

24. Go back and touch up any areas with the appropriate colors, and seal the entire box with two to three coats of high gloss varnish for maximum shine.

Chalkboard

Chalkboard

Anything can be turned into a chalkboard. By taking any wood plaque, spraying it with chalkboard paint, and adding plaster mosaics, you can create a memo board that everyone in the family will appreciate.

▼ YOU WILL NEED

- Wood plaque (any shape or size)*
- Plaster compound
- Artist's paint: Tapioca, Teddy Bear Brown*
- Artist's glaze: Mushroom, Warm Taupe, Neutral*
- Small square sponge
- Water-based wood sealer
- Satin varnish
- Chalkboard spray
- Antique gel
- Wire tool
- Brushes: sponge brush, liner brush*
- Small palette knife
- Sharp edge tool
- Medium grit sandpaper
- Pencil
- Masking tape

*Used in this project: Plaid paint, glaze; Walnut Hollow plaque; Dynasty brushes; Kemper wire tool, palette knife.

Review General Instructions, page 18, before beginning this project.

1. Seal the wood with a water-based sealer. Apply two coats, sanding between coats.

2. Use the masking tape to tape off an area for the chalkboard. Cover any exposed areas with newspaper or scrap sheets of paper. This will protect the rest of the plaque from over-spray.

3. Apply the chalkboard spray, according to the manufacturer's directions. For best results, apply two or three light coats. Allow to dry between coats. Once all coats have dried, gently pull the tape away from the surface in one smooth motion.

4. Now it is time to protect what you have just sprayed with chalkboard spray from the surrounding area, which will be painted. Tape off the chalkboard, following the painted edge so the two colors will meet.

▲**5.** Paint the plaque with two coats of Tapioca, sanding between coats. Remove the tape from the chalkboard and allow the plaque to dry.

▲**6.** Use a pencil to trace the shape of the plaque, coming in from the end approximately ½ inch. Do not worry about perfect lines; they will be covered up with plaster later. The pencil marks are only a guide.

7. Mix 1 cup of plaster compound with ½ teaspoon of Teddy Bear Brown until the colors are well blended. The small amount of brown added will tint the plaster a light warm beige.

8. Tape off the chalkboard again, so a straight edge of plaster can be made.

◄**9.** Use the palette knife to spread an even layer of plaster over the surface, carefully following the pencil mark and going slightly over the taped edge. If the project is too big, it can be done in sections. You will just have to cover the remaining plaster so it will not set up. Remember, if you go over the pencil mark, you can always sand off the excess plaster later.

10. Grabbing the top of one section of tape at a time, immediately pull the tape off of the chalkboard area. Once the tape is removed, you will be left with a straight line between the plaster and the chalkboard.

11. Allow the plaster to firm for a minute. Use the wire tool to carve your plaster mosaics. These mosaics follow the curve of the plaque with flowing lines. The pieces are carved in rows, each row following the contour of the row above it. Allow the plaster to dry completely before proceeding to the next step.

12. In a well-ventilated area or outside, use medium grit sandpaper to sand the mosaic pieces smooth. Use the wire tool to clean up any grout joints or excess plaster.

13. Mix a small amount of Warm Taupe paint with the Neutral glaze.

14. Dab a very small square of sponge into the glaze mixture and with a light tapping motion, dab the mixture onto the mosaics. Quickly work around the chalkboard. A second coat of glaze can be applied if desired.

15. Working one small area at a time, use the liner brush to paint the grout joints with Mushroom. This should be a quick brush stroke between the pieces. Do not worry about getting any glaze on the mosaic pieces.

16. Once a small area has been completed, use the sponge to wipe over the surface, wiping any excess glaze off the mosaic and feathering the color onto the surface. Most of the Mushroom glaze will still stay in the grout joints.

17. Depending on the look desired, mix more Warm Taupe paint with Neutral glaze, and again sponge over the mosaic to create a layer of subtle color. Painting the second coat of Warm Taupe glaze will give dimension to the surface and mimic tumbled marble.

18. Use a chisel brush to paint Tapioca onto the face of the area of the plaque surrounding the mosaic. This will cover any glaze that was over sponged from the previous step.

19. Use the edge of the palette knife, and run it over the edges of the plaque, taking the paint off down to the bare wood.

20. Use the same sponge as in Step 16 to apply a very small amount of antiquing gel to the areas where the paint was removed. Quickly remove the excess antiquing gel. A finger makes a great tool to rub in the color. Keep in mind that distressed areas usually occur on corners.

21. Use the clean edge of the sponge to wipe off the excess, and to even out the color.

22. Touch up any chalkboard area that may have gotten paint or plaster on it by sanding off the plaster, taping off the mosaic, and giving it a quick spray with the chalkboard paint.

23. Brush on a satin varnish, avoiding the chalkboard area.

tip **Y**ou can achieve an antique appearance by not touching up the paint after you have sanded. This gives the piece a natural aged appearance.

Mosaic Cabinet

Mosaic Cabinet

No matter what you do, the larger it is, the more intimidating it seems. I had always done small-scale projects with the plaster mosaic process, so when I was faced with the prospect of doing a large-scale piece, I was a bit worried. In the end, I realized that it wasn't a big deal. The key to success is to plan ahead, and take it one step at a time.

The first time people saw this piece, they were amazed and kept asking me where I had learned to lay mosaics. Even after they had touched the doors, they still had not caught on.

▼ YOU WILL NEED

- Wood cabinet with any number of doors*
- Plaster compound
- Artist's pigment: Pure Black, Raw Sienna*
- Artist's paint: Clover, Old Ivy, Plum Pudding, Red Violet, Licorice, Hunter Green, Barn Wood*
- Extender and thickener
- Matte varnish
- Feather
- Small square sponge
- Water-based wood sealer
- High gloss varnish
- Wire tool*
- Brushes: chisel, liner*
- Sponge brush
- Sponge brush
- Large putty knife
- Palette knife
- Medium and fine grit sandpaper
- Masking tape
- Waxed paper

*Used in this project: Walnut Hollow four door cabinet; Plaid paint, pigments; Kemper wire tool; Dynasty brushes.

Review General Instructions, page 18, before beginning this project.

1. If possible, remove all hardware and doors from the cabinet.

2. Seal the wood using a water-based sealer. After the first coat has dried, sand the surface with fine grit sandpaper. Apply a second coat.

3. With a sponge brush, paint the entire cabinet with Licorice paint. Allow the first coat to dry, sand with fine grit sandpaper, and apply a second coat of paint. Sanding between coats will give the surface a smooth finish as well as ensuring good coverage.

4. To apply the marbleized finish to the top, sponge on a mixture of Licorice, Hunter Green, Barn Wood, extender, and thickener. See Marbleizing, page 32.

5. Starting in one corner, use the feather to apply veining. Gently hold the feather in the tips of your fingers, and pull it across the surface twirling it side to side as you move. Marble veining runs in the same direction and the color fades in and out of intensity. Allow the top to dry before proceeding.

6. If the doors on the chest come off, skip to step 7. If the doors are fixed, like the ones shown in this project, tape off the frame. The less plaster that gets smeared on other areas, the less work that will have to be done later when the plaster must be sanded off.

7. For the base coat, mix 2 cups of plaster compound with 3 tablespoons of Pure Black until the color is well blended.

8. With a wide putty knife, spread a ⅛" layer of the base coat evenly over the doors of the cabinet. Don't worry about applying the plaster to areas where it should not be, it can be sanded off later.

9. If areas of the cabinet have been taped off, immediately peel off the tape. Allow the base coat to dry completely before proceeding to the next step.

10. Since this is a large project, the sanding should be done outside or in a well-ventilated area. Use medium grit sandpaper to smooth out the surface inconsistencies. Sand the area around the outside of the door to allow it to open freely. Sand the edges and corners of the cabinet doors.

11. Mix 1 cup of plaster with 1 teaspoon of Raw Sienna until the color is well blended.

12. With a large putty knife, spread a ⅛" layer of Raw Sienna plaster evenly over the base coat on two of the doors. Allow it to firm up for a minute or two before proceeding.

13. Transfer your design one door at a time. Mist the other door with water to keep it from drying out. If doing two doors at a time seems a task, do one door at a time.

14. Paint in the design. This design does not have detail; it is painted with a blocky technique. The detail comes through in the carving.

15. Use your wire tool to carve out the design, and then proceed to the background area.

16. Follow steps 11 to 15 for each door. Allow all of the doors to dry before continuing.

17. Use the wire tool to clean out the mosaic. This is where you should take your time, making sure all of the mosaic shapes are complete and the plaster is cleaned out of the grout joints.

18. Use the fine grit sandpaper to sand the surface inconsistencies, edges, and corners.

19. Use the chisel brush to touch up the colors and add any changes to the design.

20. Seal the mosaic areas with matte varnish. Seal the top, sides, and front trim with high gloss varnish.

21. Apply multiple coats to the top to enhance the marbleized appearance.

tip ▶ On large projects, you can cover portions of your project with plastic wrap and roll it back as you work. This helps keep areas from drying out before you have a chance to work on them.

Gold Table

Gold Table

It seems that in everyone's garage, attic, or spare room, there's a little table we don't know what to do with. We know that it doesn't fit just right in our home, but if we got rid of it, we would regret it later. This project uses a simple pine table. Before it was transformed, it probably wouldn't be given a second glance. Now in its painted and mosaic finery, it stands out as a one-of-a-kind piece.

You might not want to do every element of this design. You might want to mosaic the apron of the table, and leave the legs or the top bare. Or you can follow these directions to create a piece of art, rather than the simple table it originated from.

▼ YOU WILL NEED
- Wood table*
- Plaster compound
- Artist's pigment: Light Red Oxide, Yellow Ochre*
- Artist's paint: Licorice, Real Brown, Black Cherry*
- Crackle medium*
- Transfer paper
- Gold leaf kit*
- Wood sealer
- High gloss varnish
- Wire tool*
- Brushes: soft wide brush, small chisel brush, foam brush*
- Palette knife
- Putty knife
- Medium and fine grit sandpaper
- Pencil

*Used on this project: Plaid paint, pigment, crackle medium, gold leaf kit; Kemper wire tool; Walnut Hollow pine table; Dynasty brushes.

Review General Instructions, page 18, before beginning this project.

1. Seal the wood with two coats of sealer, sanding between coats.

2. Depending on the size of your furniture, mix a one-to-one ratio of Real Brown and Black Cherry paint until the colors are well blended.

3. With a soft wide brush, paint the legs and apron with two coats, sanding between coats.

4. Paint the top of the table with three to four coats, sanding between coats.

5. For the base coat, mix 1 cup of plaster compound with 2 teaspoons of Light Red Oxide until the colors are well blended.

▲**6.** Use the putty knife to spread a ⅛" base coat over the apron of the table. Wrap the plaster around the bottom edge of the apron. Don't worry about getting it on any other part of the table. It can be sanded off later. Allow the plaster to completely dry.

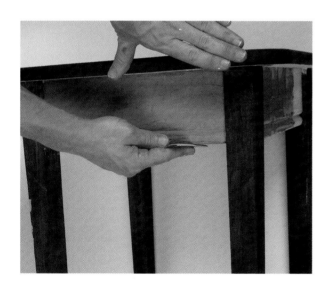

◀**7.** Sand the base coat with medium grit sandpaper. Smooth out the surface as much as possible, and continue to sand the corners and the bottom of the apron. Always use a light hand when sanding, so the sandpaper does not go through the base coat.

8. Lay the table on its side, and paint every exposed horizontal area of the legs with a generous coat of crackle medium. Allow the crackle to tack up for a minute, flip the table over onto the next side, and continue applying the crackle medium until all four sides of each leg are covered. Allow the crackle medium to dry.

tip Lying the table on its side during crackling keeps the crackle medium and paint from dripping.

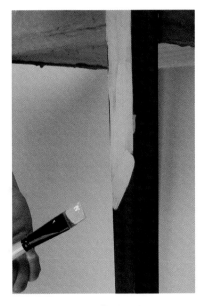  

9. Start with the first side that was coated with the crackle medium, and use a soft brush to paint the legs with Yellow Ochre. Brush in different directions, and keep the brush loaded with paint, so you don't have to re-brush an area. Allow the paint to tack up for a minute, flip the table over onto the next side, and continue applying the paint until all four sides of each leg are covered.

10. Set the table upright, and allow the paint to dry.

11. Make four copies of the design on page 116. Cut out the copies and tape them together to make a square.

12. Cut transfer paper the approximate size of the border. Tape the border design to the reverse side of the transfer paper.

13. Center the border on the top of the table, and secure each corner with a small piece of tape.

14. Use a pencil to go over the design, pressing down to transfer the design to the tabletop.

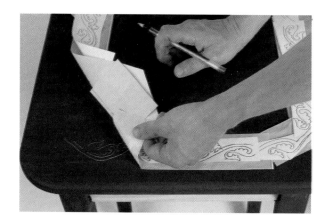

15. Lift up a corner of the design to make sure it is being transferred. If you cannot see your design, you will need to press down harder as you trace.

16. Use a small brush to paint the design with gold leaf adhesive. Apply the adhesive, making sure you paint slightly over the lines. This ensures that they will be covered with the gold leaf.

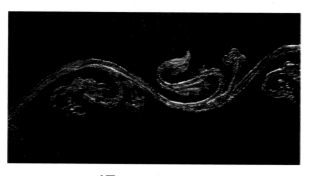
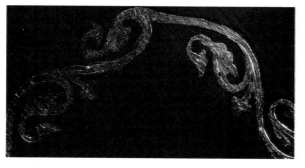

17. Allow the adhesive to tack up, and then apply the gold leaf according to the manufacturer's directions.

18. For the top coat, mix 1 cup of plaster with 1 teaspoon of Yellow Ochre until the color is well blended.

19. Use a small palette knife to apply a ⅛" top coat over the base coat, which is covering the apron of the table. Work two sides at a time, so the sides won't dry up before the table can be worked.

20. After applying the plaster on the first side, use a wire tool to carve a single row of mosaics across the bottom and random patterns across the rest of the surface. Complete the second side in the same manner.

21. Repeat steps 19 and 20 for the remaining sides. Allow the plaster to dry.

22. Use the wire tool to clean out the grout joints.

23. Use the fine grit sandpaper to smooth out the top coat.

24. Apply a light coat of gold leaf adhesive to the bottom row of mosaics on the apron of the table.

25. Apply the gold leaf according to the manufacturer's directions. Allow a little of the mosaic to show through.

26. Seal the top of the table with at least three good coats of high gloss varnish. This will protect the gold leaf from wear and tear.

27. Apply two coats of high gloss varnish to the legs and apron of the table. Allow the table to completely dry before using it.

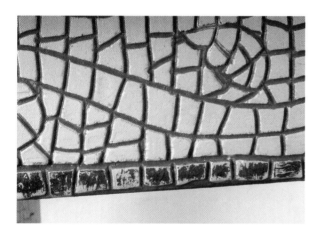

Plaster Mosaics as Art

When it comes down to it, and you have run out of things to cover with plaster mosaics, you can always turn to its most obvious use. And, that's as a quality piece of art.

"Wild Horses"

"Bird Bath"

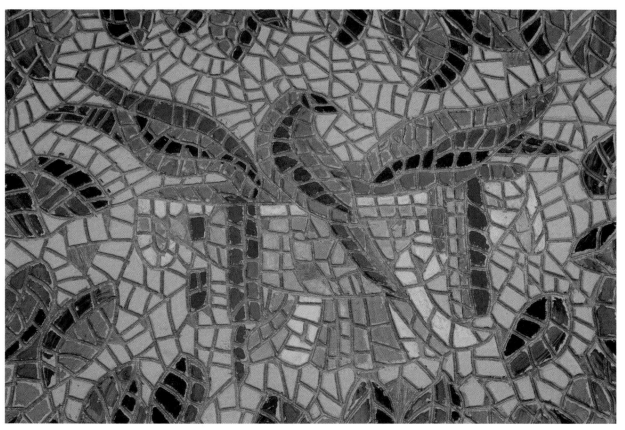

"Lady with Flute"

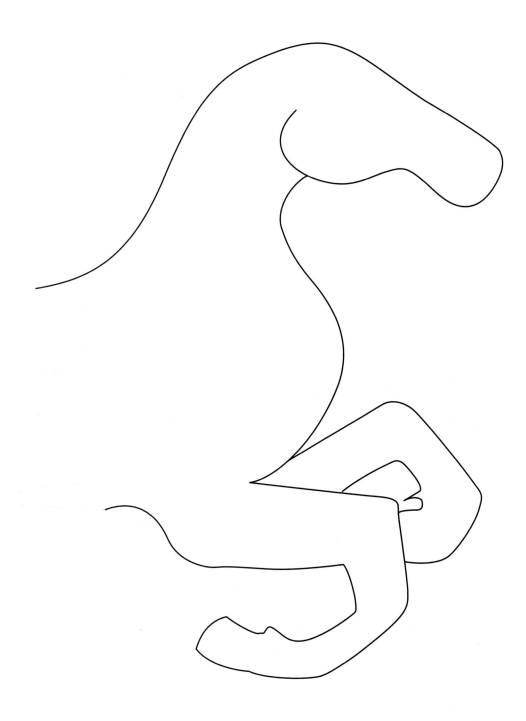

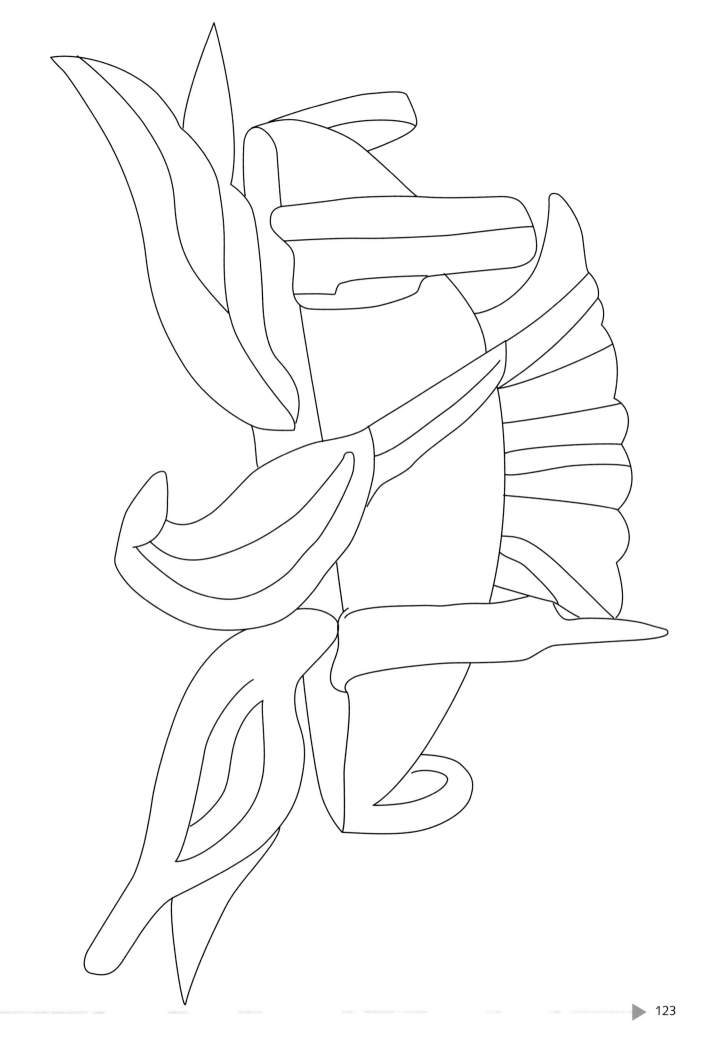

Resources

Irina Charny
19502 Sierra Santo Rd.
Irvine, CA 92612
(949) 823-9219
irina@icmosaics.com
www.icmosaics.com

FM Brush Co. Inc.
70-02 72nd Place
Glendale, NY 11385
(718) 821-5939
www.dynasty-brush.com

Kemper Tools
13595 12th Street
Chino, CA 91710
(800) 388-5367

Plaid Enterprises, Inc.
3225 Westech Drive
Norcross, GA 30092-3500
(678) 291-8100
www.plaidonline.com

Silkpaint! Corporation
P.O. Box 18
Waldron, MO 64092
(800) 563-0074
www.silkpaint.com

Walnut Hollow
1409 State Road 23
Dodgeville, WI 53533
(800) 944-2331
www.walnuthollow.com

You'll Find More Great Ideas In These Fine Books

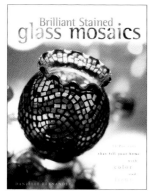

Brilliant Stained Glass Mosaics
By Danielle Fernandez
Illustrates simple mosaic techniques that can be used to create stunning, sophisticated designs for both home and garden décor. Twelve glass mosaic projects in all.
Softcover • 8½ x 11 • 128 pages
250 color illustrations
Item# 31955 • $23.99

Mosaics Made Easy
A David & Charles Craft Book
Packed with eye-catching projects presented in a modern, easy-to-follow and practical way with templates and step-by-step instructions. Provides all the information you need, including materials and techniques to guarantee success.
Softcover • 7½ x 10½ • 64 pages
56 color photos & 20 color illustrations
Item# 41185 • $12.95

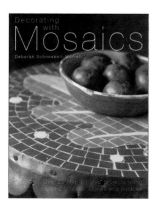

Decorating With Mosaics
By Deborah Schneebeli Morrell
Unique and colorful projects for mosaic artist of any skill level, with clear instructions and step-by-step photos.
Softcover • 8½ x 11 • 128 pages
190 color illustrations
Item# 31506 • $24.99

Easy Mosaics for Your Home and Garden
By Sarah Donnelly
These stylish and sophisticated garden mosaics are surprisingly fun and easy to make. There's no glass to cut, and no messy grouting. Simply mix, pour and embed.
Softcover • 8½ x 11 • 128 pages
200+ color illustrations
Item# 31830 • $24.99

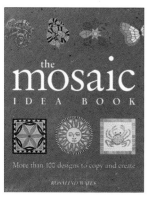

Mosaic Idea Book
By Natascha Dean
Features dozens of colorful and inspiring mosaic designs suitable for walls, floors, tables and more. Motifs range from animals, flowers and classic motifs to geometric patterns.
Softcover • 8½ x 11 • 128 pages
350 color illustrations
Item# 31746 • $24.99

Mosaics Inside and Out
Patterns and Inspirations for 17 Mosaic Projects
Doreen Mastandrea
This book makes easy the seemingly daunting task of creating mosaics for your home. Here are creative ideas and stunning projects for both interior and exterior decoration, plus the information, inspiration, and tools you need to add the colorful and sophisticated art of mosaic to kitchens, bathrooms, floors, walls, or porch and garden. Seventeen contemporary projects feature illustrated step-by-step instructions.
Softcover • 8½ x 11 • 128 pages
150 color photos
Item# 32061 • $25.00

Create Your Own Works of Art

How to Work in Stained Glass
3rd Edition
by Anita & Seymour Isenberg
One of the best-selling stained glass books ever published has been updated and revised. Includes everything that made the original the "bible" for the past 20 years, plus lots of updated and expanded information. Projects range from simple to complex for both beginners and advanced crafters. New chapters include lamp making, painting on glass, kiln firing, dichroic glass, and three-dimensional work.
Softcover • 7½ x 9 • 352 pages
500 b&w photos • 50 color photos
Item# HWSG3 • $24.95

The Complete Guide to Glues & Adhesives
by Nancy Ward & Tammy Young
In 1995, Tammy Young's The Crafter's Guide to Glues took the crafting world by storm. Now, Tammy has teamed up with Nancy Ward for this full-color follow-up that covers everything you need to know about glues and adhesives currently on the market, including their uses and applications for memory crafting, stamping, embossing, and embellishing any surface. Besides presenting the basics, like safety, there are more than 30 quick and easy step-by-step projects.
Softcover • 8¼ x 10⅞ • 144 pages
75 color photos
Item# CGTG2 ? $19.95

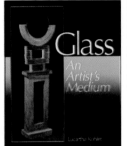

Glass: An Artist's Medium
by Lucartha Kohler
From grinding and polishing to painting and cold working, this book will teach any artist, from beginner to expert, the intricacies of forming beautiful glass sculptures. Along with an historical overview, there are chapters on glassforming with a furnace or a kiln, glass blowing, lampworking, surface decoration and more.
Hardcover • 8½ x 11 • 256 pages
190+ color photos
Item# GLASS • $34.95

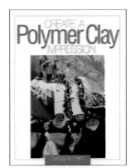

Create a Polymer Clay Impression
by Sarajane Helm
Learn how to create beautiful projects from one of today's hottest and most versatile mediums, polymer clay. Among the twenty projects in this comprehensive book are miniatures, jewelry, sewing notions and home décor, plus much more. With more than 200 photos and detailed instructions, every crafter will be inspired to create!
Softcover • 8¼ x 10⅞ • 144 pages
200+ color photos
Item# PCIMP • $23.95

The Art of Handmade Tile
by Kristin Peck
You'll create gorgeous handmade tiles quickly and easily with this new book! More than 200 photos and detailed instructions guide you through the entire process of designing, firing, decorating, and utilizing these gorgeous creations. Author Kristin Peck then shares four project ideas: culinary tiles, twig tiles, house numbers, and a mirror.
Softcover • 8¼ x 10⅞ • 144 pages
200 color photos, 50 color illustrations
Item# TBH • $21.95

The Cutting Edge
Home Dec Accents
by Vivian Peritts
If you want home décor accents that are truly on the cutting edge, just pull out your scrapbooking tools and get punching! In this new book you'll find more than 50 exciting projects for your home, including a personalized border for a teenager's room, an Asian lamp, and instructions for decorating furniture with an inlaid wood pattern. Includes detailed directions and step-by-step photographs.
Softcover • 8¼ x 10⅞ • 128 pages
225+ color photos
Item# CUTED • $19.95

Polymer: The Chameleon Clay
ArtRanch Techniques for Re-creating the Look of Ivory, Jade, Turquoise, and Other Natural Materials
by Victoria Hughes
You'll be amazed at the astounding materials you can imitate with polymer clay. By using polymer clay as your base and applying the techniques presented in this new book, you can imitate such natural materials as ivory, jade, coral, onyx, and shell. Fifteen unique and creative projects are featured, including an ivory pendant and an accordion-style jade book. A gallery of finished pieces by the author and other skilled artists will inspire you.
Softcover • 8¼ x 10⅞ • 144 pages
250 color photos and 100 illustrations
Item# ITPC • $23.95

A Beginner's Guide to Glass Engraving
by Seymour Isenberg
If you've always admired glass engraving, but thought it was too difficult or too expensive, this book is for you. The simple instructions and full-size patterns will guide you through the process so you can create works of art in glass. It's easy and not nearly as expensive as you might have thought. You'll learn everything you need to know to achieve wonderful glass engraving results, both subtle and dramatic.
Softcover • 7½ x 9 • 232 pages
125 b&w photos • 8-page color section
Item# BGGEC • $24.95